THE
PASSION
TRANSLATION

D0696719

Proverbs

WISDOM
FROM
ABOVE

Translated from the Hebrew text by

DR. BRIAN SIMMONS

tPt
BIBLE

BroadStreet
PUBLISHING

Proverbs: Wisdom from Above, The Passion Translation®
Translated from the Hebrew text by Dr. Brian Simmons

Published by BroadStreet Publishing Group, LLC
Racine, Wisconsin, USA
BroadStreetPublishing.com

© 2016 The Passion Translation®

ISBN-13: 9781424549429 (paperback)
ISBN-13: 9781424549733 (e-book)

The text of *Proverbs: Wisdom from Above*, The Passion Translation®, may be quoted up to and including thirty (30) verses without written permission from the publisher. When *Proverbs: Wisdom from Above*, The Passion Translation®, is quoted, one of the following credit lines must appear on the copyright page of the work:

> Scripture quotations marked TPT are from *Proverbs: Wisdom from Above*, The Passion Translation®, copyright © 2014, 2016. Used by permission of BroadStreet Publishing Group, LLC, Racine, Wisconsin, USA. All rights reserved. thePassionTranslation.com

> Unless otherwise indicated, all Scripture quotations are from *Proverbs: Wisdom from Above*, The Passion Translation®, copyright © 2014, 2016. Used by permission of BroadStreet Publishing Group, LLC, Racine, Wisconsin, USA. All rights reserved. thePassionTranslation.com

When Scripture quotations from TPT are used in nonsalable media, such as newsletters, transparencies, church bulletins, orders of service or similar media, it is not necessary to post a complete copyright notice, but the initials TPT must appear at the end of each quotation.

Quotations in excess of thirty (30) verses, or other permission requests must be approved in writing by BroadStreet Publishing Group, LLC. Send requests through the contact form at www.broadstreetpublishing.com/permissions. We want you to be able to use The Passion Translation and will respond to your inquiry quickly.

Cover and design by Garborg Design Works, Inc. | www.garborgdesign.com
Typesetting by Katherine Lloyd | www.theDESKonline.com

Printed in the United States of America
16 17 18 19 20   10 9 8 7 6 5 4 3

Translator's Introduction to Proverbs

AT A GLANCE

Author: Mostly Solomon, King of Israel, but other various contributors, too.

Audience: Originally Israel, but these words of wisdom are for everyone –they are written to you.

Date: Preexile (Chapters 10–29) and Postexile (Chapters 1–9, 30–31), the tenth to fifth centuries BC.

Type of Literature: Poetry and wisdom literature.

Major Themes: the fear of the Lord; God's transcendence and immanence; Godly wisdom and human foolishness; the righteous and wicked wealth and poverty; men and women; husbands and wives; Jesus and wisdom.

Outline:

ABOUT PROVERBS

The Bible is a book of poetry, not simply starched, stiff doctrines, devoid of passion. The Bible, including Proverbs, is full of poetic beauty and subtle nuances ripe with meaning. The ancient wisdom of God fills its pages!

Proverbs is a book of wisdom from above tucked inside of metaphors, symbols, and poetic imagery. God could properly be described as the divine Poet and master Artisan who crafted the cosmos to portray his glory and has given us his written Word to reveal his wisdom. Inspired from eternity, the sixty-six books of our Bible convey the full counsel and wisdom of God. Do you need wisdom? God has a verse for that!

Five books of divine poetry show us the reality of knowing God through experience, not just through history or doctrines. Job points us to the end of our self-life to discover the greatest revelation of the Lord, which is his tender love and wisdom. Psalms reveals the new life we enter into with God, expressed through praise and prayer. Next is Proverbs, where we enroll in the divine seminary of wisdom and revelation to learn the ways of God. Ecclesiastes teaches us to set our hearts not on the things of this life but on those values that endure eternally. And finally in Song of Songs, the sweetest lyrics ever composed lead us into divine romance where we are immersed in Jesus' love for his bride.

The nature of Hebrew poetry is quite different from that of English poetry. There is a pleasure found in Hebrew poetry that transcends rhyme and meter. The Hebrew verses come in a poetic package, a form of meaning that imparts an understanding that is deeper than mere logic. True revelation unfolds an encounter—an experience of knowing God as he is revealed through the mysterious vocabulary of riddle, proverb, and parable.

For example, the Hebrew word for proverb, *mashal*, has two meanings. The first is "parable, byword, metaphor, a pithy saying that expresses wisdom." But the second meaning is overlooked by many. The homonym *mashal* can also mean "to rule, to take dominion," or "to reign with power."

What you have before you now is a dynamic translation of the ancient book of Proverbs. These powerful words will bring you revelation from the throne room—the wisdom you need to guide your steps and direct your life. What you learn from these verses will change your life and launch you into your destiny.

BOOK PROFILE

Purpose

Within this divinely anointed compilation of Proverbs, there is a deep well of wisdom to reign in life and to succeed in our destiny. The wisdom that God has designed for us to receive will cause us to excel—to rise up as rulers-to-be on earth for his glory. The kingdom of God is brought into the earth as we implement the godly wisdom of Proverbs.

Although the Proverbs can be interpreted in their most literal and practical sense, the wisdom contained herein is not unlocked by a casual surface reading. The Spirit of revelation has breathed upon every verse to embed a deeper meaning of practical insight to guide our steps into the life God meant for us to live.

Author & Audience

You're about to read the greatest book of wisdom ever written, mostly penned by the wisest man to ever live. God gave his servant Solomon this wisdom to pass along to us, his servants, who continue the ministry of Jesus, the embodiment of wisdom, until he returns in full glory. While it is believed Solomon penned most of these words of wisdom, it is believed others had a hand, too, including advisers to King Hezekiah and the unknown men Agur and Lemuel—who could be pseudonyms for Solomon himself. Regardless, the one who edited the final version of Proverbs brought together the wisest teachings from the the wisest person to ever live to write a book containing some of the deepest revelation in the Bible. When Solomon pens a proverb, there is more than meets the eye!

Who are these proverbs written to? This compilation of wisdom's words is written to you! Throughout the book we find words like "Listen, my sons. Listen, my daughters." The book of Proverbs is written to us as sons and daughters of the living God. The teaching we receive is not from a distant god who tells us we'd better live right or else. These are personal words of love and tenderness from our wise Father, the Father of eternity, who speaks right into our hearts with healing, radiant words. Receive deeply the words of the kind Father of heaven as though he were speaking directly to you.

Major Themes

The kind of Hebrew wisdom found in the Proverbs is about the art of successful living. The universal appeal of these wise insights is that they touch on universal problems and issues that affect human behavior in us all. Several major themes are present in these godly wisdom sayings of God's servant Solomon:

Lady Wisdom, Revelation-Knowledge, Living-Understanding. Throughout Proverbs wisdom is personified with the metaphor of Lady Wisdom, who dispenses revelation-knowledge and living-understanding. Lady Wisdom is a figure of speech for God and His divine wisdom, who invites us to receive the best way to live, the excellent and noble way of life found. She is personified as a guide (6:22), a beloved sister or bride (7:4), and a hostess (9:1–6) who generously invites people to "come and dine at my table and drink of my wine."

In Proverbs, wisdom is inseparable from knowledge and understanding, which is not received independent of God's revelation. We are invited to "come to the one Who has living-understanding" (9:10) in order to receive what Lady Wisdom has to offer. For God promises that revelation-knowledge will flow to the one who hungers her gift of understanding (14:6).

The Fear of the Lord. From the beginning in 1:7, Proverbs makes it clear that a person gains "the essence of wisdom" and crosses "the threshold of true knowledge" only when we fear the Lord—or, as The Passion Translation translates it, we live "in complete awe and adoration of God." This theme of living in a way that our entire being worships and adores God is a constant theme throughout Proverbs.

God's Transcendence and Immanence. Proverbs teaches that God is both the Author of (transcendent) and Actor within (immanent) our human story. First, God is above and outside the world: As Creator "He broke open the hidden fountains of the deep, bringing secret springs to the surface" (3:20); "God sees everything you do and his eyes are wide open as he observes every single habit you have" (5:21); He is sovereign and steers "a king's heart for his purposes as it is for him to direct the course of a stream" (21:1).

Second, God is also apart of and involved with the world: "The rich and the poor have one thing in common: The Lord God created each one" (22:2); "The Lord champions the widow's cause" (15:25) and He "will rise to plead [the poor's] case" (22:23).

So Proverbs teaches God is all-powerful and transcendent, while also taking part in our human story as our defender and protector!

The Wise and Fool, Righteous and Wicked. Solomon believes there are basically two different kinds of people in the world: the wise righteous and wicked fools. The wise person possesses God's revelation-knowledge and living-understanding. Therefore, he is prudent, shrewd, insightful, and does what is right because he is righteous, a God-lover. This lover of God in turn is just, peaceful, upright, blameless, good, trustworthy, and kind.

The wicked fool is a completely different person. He is greedy, violent, deceitful, cruel, and speaks perversely—it's no wonder "The Lord detests the lifestyle of the wicked!" (15:9). As a foolish person, he is described as being gullible, an idiot, self-sufficient, a mocker, lazy, senseless, and rejects revelation-knowledge and living-understanding.

Many of Solomon's wise sayings relate to these two different kinds of people, teaching us how to avoid being a wicked fool and instead live as God intends us to live as his wise, righteous lovers!

Wealth and Poverty. Like many of Solomon's wise sayings, you cannot take one thought on wealth and poverty and apply it to every situation. Instead, Solomon teaches us seven major things about having wealth and being poor, and how wisdom and foolishness affect them both: the righteous are blessed with wealth by God himself; foolishness leads to poverty; fools who have wealth will soon lose it; poverty results from injustice and oppression; the wealthy are called to be generous with their wealth; gaining wisdom is far better than gaining wealth; and the value of wealth is limited.[a]

Jesus and the Church. As with the rest of the Old Testament, we are called to read Proverbs in light of Jesus and his ministry. Throughout the gospels Jesus associates himself with wisdom. For instance, in Matthew 11:18–19 Jesus claims his actions represent Lady Wisdom herself. Where he is identified with Lady Wisdom in the New Testament, it is a powerful way of saying that Jesus is the full, entire embodiment of Wisdom. In many ways Colossians 1:15–17 mirrors

a Tremper Longman III, *Proverbs*. (Grand Rapids: Baker Academic, 2006), 573-574.

Proverbs 8. Likewise, the great preface to John's gospel resonates with this same chapter when Jesus is associated with the Word, another personification of Wisdom.

The great reformer Martin Luther said, "The Scriptures must be understood in favor of Christ, not against him. For that reason they must either refer to him or must not be held to be true Scriptures." Luther understood that Jesus stood at the center of Scripture; he was found throughout Scripture, not just in the New Testament. So as you read these important words of wisdom, consider how they point to the One who perfectly embodied and is our Wisdom.

A WORD ABOUT THE PASSION TRANSLATION

We pray and trust this version of God's Word will kindle in you a burning, passionate desire for him and his heart, while impacting the church for years to come!

Get ready to be filled to overflowing with the Spirit of wisdom and the revelation that God is pouring out in this hour. Hang on to every word, for all that God says will bring life to you, a life full of his wisdom from above.

You're about to read the inspired Proverbs.

> The revelation herein will make you a champion.
> You will reign in victory and excel in life.
> Wisdom from above will pour into your heart
> Until you become an example to your generation.
> Live in this book and wisdom will live in you.

Proverbs 1

The Prologue

¹Here are kingdom revelations, words to live by,
    and words of wisdom given to empower you to reign in life,[a]
    written as proverbs by Israel's King Solomon,[b] David's son.
²Within these sayings will be found the revelation of wisdom[c]
    and the impartation of spiritual understanding.
    Use them as keys to unlock the treasures of true knowledge.
³Those who cling to these words will receive discipline
    to demonstrate wisdom in every relationship,[d]
    and to choose what is right and just and fair.
⁴These proverbs will give you great skill
    to teach the immature and make them wise,
    to give youth the understanding of their design and destiny.
⁵For the wise, these proverbs will make you even wiser,
    and for those with discernment,
    you will be able to acquire brilliant strategies for leadership.
⁶These kingdom revelations will break open your understanding

---

a 1:1 As stated in the introduction, the Hebrew word for "proverbs" means more than just a wise saying. It can also mean "to rule, to reign in power, to take dominion."

b 1:1 The name Solomon means "peaceable." There is a greater one than Solomon who gives peace to all of his followers. His name is Jesus. Solomon was the seed of David; we are the seed of Jesus Christ. Solomon had an encounter with God after asking for a discerning heart (1 Kings 3:5–14). This pleased God, so he gave Solomon wisdom, riches, and power. God is ready to impart these same things today to those who ask Him. See James 1:5–8.

c 1:2 There are six Hebrew words translated "wisdom" in the book of Proverbs. Some of them require an entire phrase in English to convey its meaning. The word used here is *chokmah*, and it is used in Proverbs forty-two times. Forty-two is the number of months Jesus ministered and the number of generations from Abraham to Christ listed in Matthew 1.

d 1:3 The Hebrew word translated "wisdom" here also means "righteousness."

to unveil the deeper meaning of parables,
poetic riddles, and epigrams,
and to unravel the words and enigmas of the wise.
[7]How then does a man gain the essence of wisdom?
We cross the threshold of true knowledge
when we live in obedient devotion to God.[a]
Stubborn know-it-alls[b] will never stop to do this,
for they scorn true wisdom and knowledge.

The Wisdom of a Father

[8]Pay close attention, my child, to your father's wise words
and never forget your mother's instructions.[c]
[9]For their insight will bring you success,
adorning you with grace-filled thoughts
and giving you reins to guide your decisions.[d]
[10]When peer pressure compels you to go with the crowd
and sinners invite you to join in,
you must simply say, "No!"

---

a 1:7 Many translations render this "the fear of the Lord." This is much more than the English concept of fear. It also implies submission, awe, worship, and reverence. The Hebrew word used here is found fourteen times in Proverbs. The number fourteen represents spiritual perfection. The number fourteen is mentioned three times in the genealogy of Jesus (Matthew 1:1–17). It is also the number for Passover. You will pass from darkness to wisdom's light by the *fear* of the Lord.

b 1:7 Or "foolish ones." There are three Hebrew words translated "fool" in Proverbs and another six that are related to a fool or foolish acts. A fool is described in Proverbs as one who hates true wisdom and correction, with no desire to acquire revelation knowledge.

c 1:8 Many expositors see this as the words of David to Solomon, yet we all must give heed to this. The words of our father (God) and our mother (the church, the freewoman) will bring us wisdom. See Galatians 4:21–31.

d 1:9 The Hebrew text here is literally translated "adornment for your head, chains for your neck." Our head is a metaphor for our thoughts, our neck a symbol for willing obedience that guides our decisions, in contrast to being stiff-necked or proud. See Philippians 2:5.

[11]When the gang says,
   "We're going to steal and kill and get away with it.
[12]We'll take down the rich and rob them.
   We'll swallow them up alive
   and take what we want from whomever we want.
[13]Then we'll take their treasures and fill our homes with loot.
[14]So come on and join us.
   Take your chance with us.
   We'll divide up all we get—
   we'll each end up with big bags of cash!"
[15]My son, refuse to go with them and stay far away from them.
[16]For crime is their way of life and bloodshed their specialty.
[17]To be aware of their snare is the best way of escape.
[18]They'll resort to murder to steal their victim's assets,
   but eventually it will be their own lives that are ambushed.
[19]In their ungodly disrespect for God
   they bring destruction on their own lives.

Wisdom's Warning

[20]Wisdom's praises are sung in the streets
   and celebrated far and wide.
[21]Yet wisdom's song is not always heard
   in the halls of higher learning.
   But in the hustle and bustle of everyday life
   its lyrics can always be heard above the din of the crowd.[a]
   You will hear wisdom's warning as she preaches courageously
   to those who stop to listen:

---

a 1:21 Literally translated, this verse reads, "Wisdom sings out in the streets and speaks her voice in the squares, crying out at the head of noisy crowds and at the entrance of the city gates." This is a parabolic statement of wisdom being heard everywhere and in every place.

22"Foolish ones, how much longer will you cling to your deception?[a]
　　How much longer will you mock wisdom,
　　cynical scorners who fight the facts?
23Come back to your senses and be restored to reality.
　　Don't even think about refusing my rebuke!
　　Don't you know that I'm ready
　　to pour out my spirit of wisdom upon you
　　and bring to you the revelation of my words
　　that will make your heart wise?
24I've called to you over and over
　　still you refuse to come to me.
　　I've pleaded with you again and again,
　　yet you've turned a deaf ear to my voice.
25Because you have laughed at my counsel
　　and have insisted on continuing in your stubbornness,
26I will laugh when your calamity comes
　　and will turn away from you at the time of your disaster.
　　Make a joke of my advice, will you?
　　Then I'll make a joke out of you!
27When the storm clouds of terror gather over your head,
　　when dread and distress consume you
　　and your catastrophe comes like a hurricane,
28You will cry out to me, but I won't answer.
　　Then it will be too late to expect my help.
　　When desperation drives you to search for me,
　　I will be nowhere to be found.
29Because you have turned up your nose at me

---

a 1:22 Or "Childish ones, how long will you love your childishness?"

and closed your eyes to the facts
and refused to worship me in awe—[a]

30Because you scoffed at my wise counsel
and laughed at my correction—

31Now you will eat the bitter fruit of your own ways.
You've made your own bed; now lie in it!
So how do you like that?

32Like an idiot you've turned away from me
and chosen destruction instead.
Your self-satisfied smugness[b] will kill you.

33But the one who always listens to me
will live undisturbed in a heavenly peace.
Free from fear, confident and courageous,
you will rest unafraid and sheltered from the storms of life.

Proverbs 2

Searching for Wisdom

1My child, will you treasure my wisdom?
Then, and only then, will you acquire it.
And only if you accept my advice
and hide it within will you succeed.

2So train your heart to listen when I speak

---

a 1:29 The Hebrew word used here can be translated "fear, dread, awe, and worship." Nearly every translation uses the word *fear* or *reverence* while ignoring the other aspects of the Aramaic word, *dekhlatha*. The New Testament is clear that there is no fear in love. See 1 John 4:18.

b 1:32 Or "your abundant prosperity."

and open your spirit wide to expand your discernment—
then pass it on to your sons and daughters.[a]
[3]Yes, cry out for comprehension and intercede for insight.
[4]For if you keep seeking it like a man would seek for sterling silver,
searching in hidden places for cherished treasure,
[5]Then you will discover the fear of the Lord
and find the true knowledge of God.
[6]Wisdom is a gift from a generous God,
and every word he speaks is full of revelation
and becomes a fountain of understanding within you.[b]
[7-8]For the Lord has a hidden storehouse of wisdom
made accessible to his godly lovers.[c]
He becomes your personal bodyguard as you follow his ways,
protecting and guarding you as you choose what is right.
[9]Then you will discover all that is just, proper, and fair,
and be empowered to make the right decisions
as you walk into your destiny.
[10]When wisdom wins your heart and revelation breaks in,
true pleasure enters your soul.
[11]If you choose to follow good counsel,
divine design will watch over you
and understanding will protect you
from making poor choices.
[12]It will rescue you from evil in disguise
and from those who speak duplicities.
[13]For they have left the highway of holiness
and walk in the ways of darkness.

---

a 2:2 As translated from the Septuagint.
b 2:6 The Septuagint adds, "found in his presence."
c 2:7–8 Or "the righteous."

¹⁴They take pleasure when evil prospers
    and thoroughly enjoy a lifestyle of sin.
¹⁵But they're walking on a path to nowhere,
    wandering away into deeper deception.

Wisdom, the Way of the Pure

¹⁶Only wisdom can save you from the flattery
    of the promiscuous woman—
    she's such a smooth-talking seductress!
¹⁷She left her husband and has forgotten her wedding vows.[a]
¹⁸You'll find her house on the road to hell,
¹⁹And all the men who go through her doors
    will never come back to the place they were—
    they will find nothing but desolation and despair.
²⁰Follow those who follow wisdom and stay on the right path.
²¹For all my godly lovers will enjoy life to the fullest
    and will inherit their destinies.[b]
²²But the treacherous ones who love darkness
    will not only lose all they could have had—
    they will lose even their own souls!

---

a 2:17 Clearly, this is a warning to those who would commit adultery, but there is a deeper meaning within this text. Proverbs tells us of two women: the adulteress and the virtuous woman of Proverbs 31. Both women speak a parable of two systems in the church. One is religious and alluring, tempting the young anointed ones to come to her "bed" of compromise (Mark 7:13). The other is the holy bride, virtuous and pure, keeping her first love ("wedding vows") for Christ alone. Her "house" is the house of the Lord. One system brings shame and despair; the other brings favor, honor, and glory. It is wisdom that protects us from one and unites us to the other. See Jeremiah 50–52 and Revelation 17–18.

b 2:21 Literally, "shall dwell in the land."

Proverbs 3

The Rewards of Wisdom

1-2My child, if you truly want a long and satisfying life,
    never forget the things that I've taught you.
    follow closely every truth that I've given you.
    Then you will have a full, rewarding life.
3Hold on to loyal love and don't let go,
    and be faithful to all that you've been taught.
    Let your life be shaped by integrity,[a]
    with truth written upon your heart.
4That's how you will find favor and understanding
    with both God and men—
    you will gain the reputation of living life well.

Wisdom's Guidance

5Trust in the Lord completely,
    and do not rely on your own opinions.
    With all your heart rely on him to guide you,
    and he will lead you in every decision you make.
6Become intimate with him in whatever you do,
    and he will lead you wherever you go.[b]
    Don't think for a moment that you know it all,[c]
7For wisdom comes when you adore him with undivided devotion
    and avoid everything that's wrong—

---

a 3:3 Or "tie them around your neck." The neck is a symbol of our will and conscience.
b 3:6 Or "He will cut a straight path before you."
c 3:6 We should always be willing to listen to correction and instruction.

[8]For then you will find the healing refreshment
   your body and spirit long for.[a]
[9]Glorify God with all your wealth,
   honoring him with your very best,[b]
   with every increase that comes to you.
[10]Then every dimension of your life will overflow with blessings
   from an uncontainable source of inner joy!

Wisdom's Correction

[11]My child, when the Lord God speaks to you,
   never take his words lightly,
   and never be upset when he corrects you.
[12]For the Father's discipline comes only
   from his passionate love and pleasure for you.
   Even when it seems like his correction is harsh,
   it's still better than any father on earth gives to his child.
[13]Those who find true wisdom obtain the tools for understanding,
   the proper way to live,[c]
   for they will have a fountain of blessing pouring into their lives.
   To gain the riches of wisdom is far greater
   than gaining the wealth of the world.
[14]As wisdom increases, a great treasure is imparted,
   greater than many bars of refined gold.

---

a 3:8 Literally, "healing to your navel and moistening to your bones." The blood supply for
  a baby in the womb comes through the navel. New cells are made in the marrow of our
  bones. As the navel and bones picture the life flow of our bodies, so the navel and bones
  are a picture of our inner being. See John 7:37–39.
b 3:9 Or "the firstfruits."
c 3:13 The Hebrew-Aramaic text here implies that wisdom gives the ability to take raw
  facts and draw right conclusions and meaning from them.

¹⁵It is a more valuable commodity than gold and gemstones,[a]
for there is nothing you desire that could compare to her!
¹⁶Wisdom extends to you long life in one hand
and wealth and promotion[b] in the other.
Out of her mouth flows righteousness,
and her words release both law and mercy.[c]
¹⁷The ways of wisdom are sweet,
always drawing you into the place of wholeness.[d]
¹⁸Seeking for her brings the discovery of untold blessings,
for she is the healing tree of life to those who taste her fruits.[e]

Wisdom's Blueprints

¹⁹The Lord laid the earth's foundations with wisdom's blueprints.
By his living-understanding all the universe came into being.[f]
²⁰By his divine revelation he broke open
the hidden fountains of the deep,
bringing secret springs to the surface
as the mist of the night dripped down from heaven.[g]

Wisdom, Our Hiding Place

²¹My child, never drift off course from these two goals for your life:

---

a 3:15 The Hebrew word translated as "gemstones" here can also refer to rubies, coral, or pearls.

b 3:16 Or "honor."

c 3:16 The Septuagint adds this last sentence, which is not found in the Hebrew.

d 3:17 The Hebrew word translated as "wholeness" here can also mean "peace" or "prosperity."

e 3:18 Verses 17 and 18 are recited in contemporary Torah services as the Torah scroll is returned to the ark, where it is kept.

f 3:19 When compared with Colossians 1:16, we can see that Wisdom is used as a title in Proverbs for the Living Wisdom, Jesus Christ. See also 1 Corinthians 1:30.

g 3:20 The dew is a metaphor of the Holy Spirit, who comes from the heavens and drenches us with God's presence. See Genesis 27:28, Deuteronomy 32:2, Psalm 133:3, and Judges 6:37–40.

To walk in wisdom and to discover discernment.[a]
Don't ever forget how they empower you.
22For they strengthen you inside and out
and inspire you to do what's right;[b]
you will be energized and refreshed by the healing they bring.
23They give you living hope to guide you,
and not one of life's tests will cause you to stumble.
24You will sleep like a baby, safe and sound—
your rest will be sweet and secure.
25You will not be subject to terror, for it will not terrify you.
Nor will the disrespectful be able to push you aside,[c]
26Because God is your confidence in times of crisis,
keeping your heart at rest in every situation.[d]

Wisdom in Relationships

27Why would you withhold payment on your debt[e]
when you have the ability to pay? Just do it![f]
28When your friend comes to ask you for a favor,
why would you say, "Perhaps tomorrow,"
when you have the money right there in your pocket?
Help him today!

---

a 3:21 Like many Hebrew words, there are various possible translations. The word translated as "discernment" here can also mean "discretion, counsel, meditation, and purpose."

b 3:22 Or "adorn your neck." The neck is a picture of our will and conscience.

c 3:25 As translated from the Septuagint.

d 3:26 Or "keeping your foot from being caught."

e 3:27 The LXX is "Why would withhold from the poor (those who need it)."

f 3:27 The Hebrew text here literally means "Do not withhold *wealth* from its owners." See
Romans 13:7.

[29]Why would you hold a grudge[a] in your heart
    toward your neighbor who lives right next door?
[30]And why would you quarrel with those
    who have done nothing wrong to you?
    Is that a chip on your shoulder?[b]
[31]Don't act like those bullies or learn their ways.
[32]Every violent thug is despised by the Lord,
    but every tender lover finds friendship with God
    and will hear his intimate secrets.[c]
[33]The wicked walk under God's constant curse,
    but godly lovers walk under a stream of his blessing,
    for they seek to do what is right.
[34]If you walk with the mockers you will learn to mock,
    but God's grace and favor flow to the meek.[d]
[35]Stubborn fools fill their lives with disgrace,
    but glory and honor rest upon the wise.

Proverbs 4

A Father's Instruction

[1]Listen to my correction, my sons,
    for I speak to you as your father.[e]
    Let discernment enter your heart
    and you will grow wise with the understanding I impart.

---

a 3:29 Or "plot evil."
b 3:30 See Romans 12:18.
c 3:32 See Psalm 25:14.
d 3:34 See James 4:6 and 1 Peter 5:5.
e 4:1 Read and study this entire chapter as though it were Jesus Christ speaking to you.
   He is the everlasting Father and we are called his sons. See Isaiah 9:6–7 and Revelation
   21:6–7.

[2]My revelation truth[a] is a gift to you,
    so remain faithful to my instruction.
[3]For I, too, was once the delight of my father[b]
    and cherished by my mother, their beloved child.[c]
[4]Then my father taught me, saying:
    "Never forget my words.
    If you do everything that I teach you, you will reign in life."[d]
[5]So make wisdom your quest—
    search for the revelation of life's meaning.
    Don't let what I say go in one ear and out the other.
[6]Stick with wisdom and she will stick to you,
    protecting you throughout your days.
    She will rescue all those who passionately listen to her voice.[e]
[7]Wisdom is the most valuable commodity—so buy it!
    Revelation knowledge is what you need—so invest in it!
[8]Wisdom will exalt you when you exalt her truth.[f]
    She will lead you to honor and favor
    when you live your life by her insights.
[9]You will be adorned with beauty and grace,[g]
    and wisdom's glory will wrap itself around you,[h]
    making you victorious in the race.

---

a 4:2 Literally, "Torah."

b 4:3 See Matthew 17:5 and John 3:35.

c 4:3 Or "unique." See Luke 1–2.

d 4:4 The lessons of wisdom are meant to be passed on from parents to children.

e 4:6 It is not enough to acquire wisdom; we must love her and listen wholeheartedly to her instruction.

f 4:8 The Septuagint says, "Build a fort for wisdom and she will lift you high."

g 4:9 Literally, "She will place a garland of grace on your head and a crown of beauty upon you." A garland and a crown are metaphors for what is awarded a victor in a race. See 1 Corinthians 9:24.

h 4:9 Or "wisdom's laurel of glory shielding you."

Two Pathways

[10]My sons, if you will take the time to stop and listen to me
    and embrace what I say,
    you will live a long and happy life
    full of understanding in every way.
[11]I have taken you by the hand in wisdom's ways,
    pointing you to the path of integrity.
[12]Your progress will have no limits when you come along with me,
    and you will never stumble as you walk along the way.
[13]So receive my correction[a] no matter how hard it is to swallow,
    for wisdom will snap you back into place—
    her words will be invigorating life to you.
[14]Do not detour into darkness or even set foot on that path.
[15]Stay away from it; don't even go there!
[16]For troublemakers are restless if they are not involved in evil.
    They are not satisfied until they have brought someone harm.
[17]They feed on darkness and drink
    until they're drunk on the wine of wickedness.[b]
[18]But the lovers of God walk on the highway of light,[c]
    and their way shines brighter and brighter
    until they bring forth the perfect day.
[19]But the wicked walk in thick darkness,
    like those who travel in fog
    and yet don't have a clue why they keep stumbling!

---

a 4:13 Wisdom will correct us and adjust our hearts to discipline. We must embrace the corrections of wisdom in order to mature spiritually.

b 4:17 Or "violence."

c 4:18 Or "the glow of sunlight."

Healing Words

[20]Listen carefully, my dear child, to everything that I teach you,
    and pay attention to all that I have to say.
[21]Fill your thoughts with my words
    until they penetrate deep into your spirit.[a]
[22]Then, as you unwrap my words,[b]
    they will impart true life and radiant health
    into the very core of your being.
[23]So above all, guard the affections of your heart,[c]
    for they affect all that you are.
    Pay attention to the welfare of your innermost being,
    for from there flows the wellspring of life.
[24]Avoid dishonest speech and pretentious words.
    Be free from using perverse words no matter what!

Watch Where You're Going

[25]Set your gaze on the path before you.
    With fixed purpose, looking straight ahead,
    ignore life's distractions.[d]
[26]Watch where you're going!
    Stick to the path of truth,
    and the road will be safe and smooth before you.
[27]Don't allow yourself to be sidetracked for even a moment,
    or take the detour that leads to darkness.

---

a 4:21 See Colossians 3:16.
b 4:22 Or "discover my words."
c 4:23 The Hebrew word, levav, is the most common word for heart. It includes our
    thoughts, our will, our discernment, and our affections.
d 4:25 Implied in the text. See also Hebrews 12:1–2.

Proverbs 5

Avoid Promiscuity

¹Listen to me, my son,
> for I know what I'm talking about.
> Listen carefully to my advice
²So that wisdom and discernment will enter your heart,
> and then the words you speak will express what you've learned.
³Remember this:
> The lips of a seductress seem sweet like honey,
> and her smooth words are like music in your ears.[a]
⁴But I promise you this:
> In the end all you'll be left with is a bitter conscience.[b]
> For the sting of your sin will pierce your soul like a sword.
⁵She will ruin your life, drag you down to death,
> and lead you straight to hell.[c]
⁶She has prevented many from considering the paths of life.
> Yes, she will take you with her where you don't want to go,
> sliding down a slippery road
> and not even realizing where the two of you will end up!
⁷Listen to me, young men,
> and don't forget this one thing I'm telling you—
> run away from her as fast as you can!

---

a 5:3 Some Jewish expositors view this "promiscuous woman" as a metaphor for heresy. She seduces, deceives, and drags to hell. For the believer, the promiscuous woman can be a picture of the false anointing of the religious spirit that attempts to seduce us, weaken our message, and rob the anointing of God from our ministries. Of course, there is also a clear and dire warning for all to stay sexually pure or face the consequences.

b 5:4 Or "bitter as wormwood." See Revelation 8:10–11.

c 5:5 Or "Sheol." This is the Aramaic and Hebrew word for the place of the dead. The Greeks call it Hades. Sheol is not eternal; it will be destroyed. See Hosea 13:14 and Revelation 20:4.

[8]Don't even go near the door of her house
   unless you want to fall into her seduction.
[9]In disgrace you will relinquish your honor to another,
   and all your remaining years will be squandered—
   given over to the cruel one.[a]
[10]Why would you let strangers take away your strength[b]
   while the labors of your house go to someone else?
[11]For when you grow old you will groan in anguish and shame[c]
   as sexually transmitted diseases consume your body.[d]
[12]And then finally you'll admit that you were wrong and say,
   "If only I had listened to wisdom's voice
   and not stubbornly demanded my own way,
   because my heart hated to be told what to do!
[13]Why didn't I take seriously the warning of my wise counselors?
   Why was I so stupid to think that I could get away with it?
[14]Now I'm totally disgraced and my life is ruined!
   I'm paying the price—
   for the people of the congregation are now my judges."[e]

Sex Reserved for Marriage

[15]My son, share your love with your wife alone.
   Drink from her well of pleasure and from no other.
[16]Why would you have sex with a stranger,
   or with anyone other than her?

---

a 5:9 This would be the Devil, who torments the conscience as the result of this sin.

b 5:10 Or "wealth." This could also refer to spiritual strength and wealth.

c 5:11 The Hebrew word translated as "groan" here is also used for the roar of a lion or the ocean's roar.

d 5:11 Implied in the context of the topic of sexual promiscuity. The Hebrew word her means "diseases."

e 5:14 See John 8:1–11.

[17]Reserve this pleasure for you and her alone and not with another.[a]
[18]Your sex life will be blessed[b]

as you take joy and pleasure in the wife of your youth.
[19]Let her breasts be your satisfaction,[c]

and let her embrace[d] intoxicate you at all times.

Be continually delighted and ravished with her love!
[20]My son, why would you be exhilarated by an adulteress—

by embracing a woman[e] who is not yours?
[21]For God sees everything you do and his eyes are wide open

as he observes every single habit you have.
[22]Beware that your sins don't overtake you

and the scars of your own conscience

become the ropes that tie you up.
[23]Those who choose wickedness die for lack of self-control,

for their foolish ways lead them astray,

carrying them away as hostages—

kidnapped captives robbed of destiny.[f]

---

a 5.17 Because of the sudden change in the Hebrew text to the masculine gender ("stranger" or "another"), there is an inference that men having sex with men is forbidden, as well as sex with a woman who is not your wife.

b 5:18 The Hebrew phrase used here includes the word *fountain*, which is an obvious metaphor for the sex act. The root word for *fountain* can also refer to the eyes. It may be a poetic subtlety that the eyes should only be on your wife, not on the nakedness of another. See verse 19.

c 5:19 The Hebrew includes a picturesque metaphor of the wife being like a "friendly deer and a favored filly."

d 5:19 The Septuagint reads, "Let her share conversation with you."

e 5:20 Or "breasts."

f 5:23 Implied in the context.

Proverbs 6

Words of Wisdom

[1]My son, if you cosign a loan for an acquaintance
    and guarantee his debt,
    you'll be sorry that you ever did it!
[2]You'll be trapped by your promise
    and legally bound by the agreement.
    So listen carefully to my advice—
[3]Quickly get out of it if you possibly can!
    Swallow your pride, get over your embarrassment
    and go tell your "friend" you want your name[a] off that contract.
[4]Don't put it off, and don't rest until you get it done.
[5]Rescue yourself from future pain[b]
    and be free from it once and for all.
    You'll be so relieved that you did![c]

Life Lessons

[6]When you're feeling lazy,
    come and learn a lesson from this tale of the tiny ant.
    Yes, all you lazybones come learn
    from the example of the ant and enter into wisdom.
[7]The ant has no chief, no boss, no manager—
    no one has to tell them what to do.

---

a 6:3 There is an implication in the Hebrew that the one whose loan was cosigned for is
    no longer a friend. The Hebrew word can also be translated "apostate."
b 6:5 Implied in the context. The Hebrew word means "trap."
c 6:5 The life lesson to learn is that even when considering something that seems to
    be good, there may be unexpected consequences that should be considered before
    obligating yourself.

⁸You'll see them working and toiling all summer long,
   stockpiling their food in preparation for winter.
⁹So wake up, sleepyhead. How long will you lie there?
   When will you wake up and get out of bed?
¹⁰If you keep nodding off and thinking, I'll do it later,
   or say to yourself I'll just sit back awhile and take it easy,
   just watch how the future unfolds!
¹¹By making excuses you'll learn what it means to go without.
   Poverty will pounce on you like a bandit[a]
   and move in as your roommate for life.[b]
¹²⁻¹³Here's another life lesson to learn
   from observing the wayward and wicked man.[c]
   You can tell they are lawless.
   They're constant liars, proud deceivers,
   full of clever ploys and convincing plots.[d]
¹⁴Their twisted thoughts are perverse,
   always with a scheme to stir up trouble,
   and sowing strife with every step they take.
¹⁵But when calamity comes knocking on their door,

---

a 6:11 Or "vagabond." The Hebrew phrase here is literally translated "one who walks (away)."

b 6:11 The life lesson from Solomon's parable is this: The ant only lives six months yet stores more food than it will ever consume. We should learn the wisdom of preparing for the future and learn frugality in the present. Don't put off for the future the preparations you should make today. Now is always better than later. Today is the day to choose what's right and serve the Lord.

c 6:12–13 The Hebrew word translated "wayward and lawless" is actually "a man of Belial." This is a metaphor for a worthless man who worships other gods. The name Belial is found in numerous Dead Sea scrolls as a term for Satan.

d 6:12–13 The Hebrew gives a picture of those who "wink their eyes, shuffle their feet, and point their fingers." This is a figure of speech for the devious ways of the wicked.

suddenly and without warning they're undone—
broken to bits, shattered, with no hope of healing.[a]

Seven Things God Hates

[16]There are six evils God truly hates
and a seventh[b] that is an abomination to him:
[17]Putting others down while considering yourself superior,
spreading lies and rumors,
spilling the blood of the innocent,
[18]Plotting evil in your heart toward another,
gloating over doing what's plainly wrong,
[19]Spouting lies in false testimony,
and stirring up strife between friends.[c]
These are entirely despicable to God![d]
[20]My son, obey your father's godly instruction
and follow your mother's life-giving teaching.[e]
[21]Fill your heart with their advice
and let your life be shaped by what they've taught you.[f]
[22]Their wisdom will guide you wherever you go
and keep you from bringing harm to yourself.
Their instruction will whisper to you at every sunrise
and direct you through a brand new day.

---

a 6:15 The life lesson here is this: The clever and devious may look like they're getting ahead in life, but their path guarantees destruction, with no one to help them out of it.

b 6:16 The number seven is the number of fullness and completion. The poetic form here is stating that evil in its fullness is an abomination to God. The seven things are a description of the sin of man that stands in the temple of our bodies attempting to usurp God.

c 6:19 The Aramaic is "deception among brothers."

d 6:19 A summary statement implied in the context.

e 6:20 For the New Testament believer, our mother is the church, who nurtures us and feeds us life-giving words. See Galatians 4:21–31.

f 6:21 Or "bind their words on your heart and tie them around your neck."

[23] For truth[a] is a bright beam of light
   shining into every area of your life,
   instructing and correcting you
   to discover the ways to godly living.

Truth or Consequences

[24-25] Truth will protect you from immorality
   and from the promiscuity of another man's wife.
   Your heart won't be enticed by her flatteries[b]
   or lust over her beauty—
   nor will her suggestive ways conquer you.
[26] Prostitutes reduce a man to poverty,[c]
   and the adulteress steals your soul—
   she may even cost you your life![d]
[27] For how can a man light his pants on fire and not be burned?
[28] Can he walk over hot coals of fire[e] and not blister his feet?
[29] What makes you think that you can sleep with another man's wife
   and not get caught?
   Do you really think you'll get away with it?
   Don't you know it will ruin your life?
[30] You can almost excuse a thief if he steals to feed his own family.
[31] But if he's caught, he still has to pay back what he stole sevenfold;
   his punishment and fine will cost him greatly.
[32] Don't be so stupid as to think
   you can get away with your adultery.

---

a 6:23 Or "Torah."
b 6:24-25, Or "Don't let her captivate you with her fluttering eyelids."
c 6:26 Or "beg for a loaf of bread."
d 6:26 The Hebrew phrase here is literally translated, "She hunts for your precious soul."
e 6:28 A picture of the lusts of the flesh.

It will destroy your life,[a] and you'll pay the price
   for the rest of your days.
33 You'll discover what humiliation, shame,
   and disgrace are all about,
   for no one will ever let you forget what you've done.
34 A husband's jealousy makes a man furious;
   he won't spare you when he comes to take revenge.
35 Try all you want to talk your way out of it—
   offer him a bribe and see if you can manipulate him
   with your money.
   Nothing will turn him aside
   when he comes to you with vengeance in his eyes!

Proverbs 7

Wisdom, Your True Love

1 Stick close to my instruction, my son,
   and follow all my advice.
2 If you do what I say you will live well.
   Guard your life with my revelation-truth,
   for my teaching is as precious as your eyesight.[b]
3 Treasure my instructions, and cherish them within your heart.[c]
4 Say to wisdom, "I love you."
   And to understanding, "You're my sweetheart."
5 "May the two of you protect me, and may we never be apart!"

---

a 6:32 Or "The destroyer of his soul will do this."
b 7:2 Or "like you would the pupil of your eye," Literally, "the little man of the eye," which
   is a figure of speech for your most prized possession.
c 7:3 Or "Write them upon the tablets of your heart."

For they will keep you from the adulteress
with her smooth words meant to seduce your heart.
⁶Looking out the window of my house one day
⁷I noticed among the mindless crowd
a simple, naïve young man who was about to go astray.
⁸There he was, walking down the street.
Then he turned the corner,
going on his way as he hurried on to the house of the harlot—
the woman he had planned to meet.
⁹There he was in the twilight as darkness fell,
convinced no one was watching
as he entered the black shadows of hell.ᵃ
¹⁰That's when their rendezvous began.
A woman of the night appeared,
dressed to kill the strength of any man.
She was decked out as a harlot, pursuing her amorous plan.
¹¹Her voice was seductive, rebellious, and boisterous
as she wandered far from what's right.

---

a 7:9 Implied from verse 27.

¹²Her type can be found soliciting on street corners
    on just about any night.ᵃ
¹³So she wrapped her arms around the senseless young man
    and held him tight—
    she enticed him with kisses which seemed so right.
    Then, with insolence, she whispered in his ear,
¹⁴"Come with me. It'll be all right.
    I've got everything we need for a feast.
    I'll cook you a wonderful dinner.ᵇ
    So here I am—I'm all yours!
¹⁵You're the very one I've looked for,
    the one I knew I wanted from the moment I saw you.
    That's why I've come out here tonight,
    so I could meet a man just like you.ᶜ
¹⁶I've spread my canopy bed with coverings,

---

a 7:12 This parable not only warns against the obvious evils of adultery and immorality, but also serves as a warning to the anointed young men in ministry not to be seduced by the religious system. Wisdom looks from the window (revelation and insight—Ezekiel 8) of her house (the true church of Jesus) and sees a young man (not fully mature—1 John 2:12–14) who has placed himself in the path of sin. This made him vulnerable to the seduction of the "harlot" system of a works-based religion that enticed him into her bed (partnership, covering, and ordination with her and her system—Revelation 17–18) covered with Egyptian linens (Egypt is a picture of the world system that holds people in bondage). She is loud and stubborn (the old self-life never dealt with) and will not remain in her house (the true church of Jesus). She lives in the darkness of compromise and her ways are the ways of death. She doesn't remain faithful to her husband (the Bridegroom-God). The two women of Proverbs are the harlot mentioned here and the virtuous woman found in chapter 31, who speak of two systems of worship. One is true and virtuous; the other is false and seductive.

b 7:14 Or "offered peace offerings and paid my vows [in the Temple]." This is a way of saying, "I have lots of meat left over from the sacrifices I've offered, enough for a great meal."

c 7:15 Compared to Song of Songs 3:1–4, this seems to be a parodic reversal of the Shulamite who goes out into the city to seek a man, and when she finds him, embraces him. This account of the harlot seems to be the converse of the theme of Song of Songs.

lovely multicolored Egyptian linens spread
and ready for you to lie down on.
¹⁷I've sprinkled the sheets with intoxicating perfume
made from myrrh, aloes, and sweet cinnamon.^a
¹⁸Come, let's get comfortable and take pleasure in each other
and make love all night!
¹⁹There's no one home, for my husband's away on business.
²⁰He left home loaded with money to spend,
so don't worry.
He won't be back until another month ends."^b
²¹⁻²²He was swayed by her sophistication,
enticed by her longing embrace.
She led him down the wayward path right into sin and disgrace.
So quickly he went astray with no clue
where he was truly headed,
taken like a dumb ox alongside of the butcher.
She was like a venomous snake coiled to strike,
so she set her fangs into him!^c
²³He 's like a man about to be executed with an arrow
right through his heart—
like a bird that flies into the net,
unaware of what's about to happen.
²⁴So listen to me, you young men.
You'd better take my words seriously!

---

a 7:17 Although these spices are found in the sacred anointing oil, the adulteress
(religious system) has only a false anointing, with no true power.
b 7:20 Or "He left with a bag of money and won't be back until the new moon."
c 7:21–22 This last sentence is arguably a difficult verse to translate with many variant
options. The Aramaic is "taken like a dog to captivity." The Hebrew can be translated
"bounding like a stag to a trap." Other ancient Jewish commentaries refer to this portion
as "rushing like a venomous snake to discipline the foolish one," meaning that with the
swiftness of a snake striking its prey, a fool lunges into his own destruction.

²⁵Control your sexual urges and guard your hearts from lust.
   Don't let your passions get out of hand
   and don't lock your eyes onto a beautiful woman.
   Why would you want to even get close
   to temptation and seduction,
   to have an affair with her?
²⁶She has pierced the souls of multitudes of men—
   many mighty ones have fallen
   and have been brought down by her.ᵃ
²⁷If you're looking for the road to hell,
   just go looking for her house!

Proverbs 8

Wisdom Calling

¹⁻³Can't you hear the voice of wisdom?ᵇ
   From the top of the mountains of influence
   she speaks into the gateways of the glorious city.ᶜ
   At the place where pathways merge,
   at the entrance of every portal,
   there she stands, ready to impart understanding,

---

a 7:26 The Aramaic is even more descriptive: "She has slain a multitude of mighty ones; they've all been killed by her."

b 8:1–3 Wisdom is personified throughout the book of Proverbs. Lady Wisdom is a figure of speech for God himself, who invites us to receive the best way to live, the excellent and noble way of life found in Jesus Christ. Jesus is wisdom personified, for he was anointed with the Spirit of wisdom. See 1 Corinthians 1:30, Colossians 2:3, and Isaiah 11:1–2.

c 8:1–3 As translated from the Aramaic. The church is also a gateway, the house of God, the portal to heaven, that Jesus calls a "city set on a hill." Christ is the head of the church, where the wisdom of God is revealed. See 1 Corinthians 1 and Ephesians 3:10–12.

shouting aloud to all who enter,
preaching her sermon to those who will listen.*a*
4"I'm calling to you, sons of Adam,
yes, and to you daughters as well.*b*
5Listen to me and you will be prudent and wise.
For even the foolish and feeble
can receive an understanding heart
that will change their inner being.*c*
6The meaning of my words will release within you revelation
for you to reign in life.*d*
My lyrics will empower you to live by what is right.
7For everything I say is unquestionably true,
and I refuse to endure the lies of lawlessness—
my words will never lead you astray
8All the declarations of my mouth can be trusted;
they contain no twisted logic or perversion of the truth.
9All my words are clear and straightforward to everyone
who possesses spiritual understanding.
If you have an open mind, you will receive revelation-knowledge.
10My wise correction is more valuable than silver or gold.
The finest gold is nothing compared to the
revelation-knowledge I can impart.

---

a 8:1–3 In chapter 7 it was the harlot calling out to the simple; here it is Lady Wisdom. True wisdom is easy to find—we only have to listen to her voice. Though it comes from above, it is found on street level. Creation and conscience are two voices that speak to our hearts. To discover wisdom we don't need a brilliant intellect but a tender, attentive heart.

b 8:4 Implied in the text.

c 8:5 Implied in the text.

d 8:6 The Hebrew word is literally translated as "princely" or "noble" things. The implication is that these words of wisdom are for ruling and reigning in life.

¹¹Wisdom is so priceless that it exceeds the value of any jewel.^a
Nothing you could wish for can equal her.
¹²For I am wisdom, and I am shrewd and intelligent.
I have at my disposal living-understanding
to devise a plan for your life.^b
¹³Wisdom pours into you
when you begin to hate every form of evil in your life,
for that's what worship and fearing God is all about.
Then you will discover
that your pompous pride and perverse speech
are the very ways of wickedness that I hate!

The Power of Wisdom

¹⁴"You will find true success when you find me,
for I have insight into wise plans that are designed just for you!
I hold in my hands living-understanding, courage, and strength.
They're all ready and waiting for you.
¹⁵I empower kings to reign^c and rulers to make laws that are just.
¹⁶I empower princes to rise and take dominion,
and generous ones to govern the earth.^d
¹⁷I will show my love to those who passionately love me.^e
For they will search and search continually until they find me.
¹⁸Unending wealth and glory
come to those who discover where I dwell.

---

a 8:11 Literally, "corals" or "pearls."
b 8:12 Or "to discover clever inventions."
c 8:15 We have been made kings and priestly rulers by the grace of redemption.
d 8:16 As translated from many Hebrew manuscripts and the Septuagint. Other Hebrew manuscripts have, "and all nobles who govern justly." The word *nobles* can also be translated "generous ones."
e 8:17 Wisdom is not found by the halfhearted. One must love wisdom to gain it. A superficial desire will only yield a superficial knowledge.

The riches of righteousness and a long, satisfying life
   will be given to them.[a]
[19]What I impart has greater worth than gold and treasure.
   and the increase I bring benefits more than a windfall of income.
[20]I lead you into the ways of righteousness,
   to discover the paths of true justice.
[21]Those who love me gain great wealth[b] and a glorious inheritance,
   and I will fill their lives with treasures.

Wisdom in the Beginning

[22]"In the beginning I was there,
   for God possessed me[c] even before he created the universe.
[23]From eternity past I was set in place,
   before the world began.
   I was anointed from the beginning.[d]
[24]Before the oceans depths were poured out,
   and before there were any glorious fountains
   overflowing with water,[e]
   I was there, dancing![f]

---

a 8:18 Or "riches and righteousness." The phrase "a long, satisfying life" is from the Aramaic.

b 8:21 The Aramaic is "I will leave great hope as an inheritance to my friends."

c 8:22 The Aramaic and the Septuagint read, "The Lord created me at the beginning." The Hebrew verb translated here as "possessed" has two basic meanings. One is "acquired"; the other is "created." Poetically, it is a statement that the existence of Wisdom (Christ) was not independent of God at creation but was manifested and possessed by God as he created all things. Otherwise, it would sound like God was without wisdom before he created it.

d 8:23 The Hebrew word translated "anointed" here literally means "poured out" and is often used to describe the anointing oil poured out over a king.

e 8:24 The Hebrew uses the word kabad, which means "glory," in describing the fountains. It could also be translated "fountains of glory" or "glorious fountains."

f 8:24 Many translation have "I was born (or brought forth)." The Hebrew word for "born" is taken from a word that means "to kick and twirl" or "to dance."

²⁵Even before one mountain had been sculpted
　　or one hill raised up,
　　I was already there, dancing!
²⁶When he created the earth, the fields,
　　even the first atom of dust,
　　I was already there.
²⁷When he hung the tapestry of the heavens
　　and stretched out the horizon of the earth,
²⁸When the clouds and skies were set in place
　　and the subterranean fountains began to flow strong,
　　I was already there.
²⁹When he set in place the pillars of the earth
　　and spoke the decrees of the seas,
　　commanding the waves
　　so that they wouldn't overstep their boundaries,
³⁰I was there, close to the Creator's side[a] as his master artist.[b]
　　Daily he was filled with delight in me
　　as I playfully rejoiced before him.[c]
³¹I laughed and played,
　　so happy with what he had made,
　　while finding my delight in the children of men.[d]

Wisdom Worth Waiting For

³²"So listen, my sons and daughters to everything I tell you,
　　for nothing will bring you more joy than following my ways.

---

a 8:30 See John 1:1.

b 8:30 Or "architect."

c 8:30 The Hebrew word translated here as "rejoicing" can also be translated as "joyfully playing" or "laughing."

d 8:31 What a beautiful picture we find here of Wisdom (Christ), who finds his fulfillment in us. See also Psalm 8:4–9 and 16:3, and Ephesians 2:10 and 19–22.

[33]Listen to my counsel,
    for my instruction will enlighten you.
    You'll be wise not to ignore it.
[34]If you wait at wisdom's doorway,[a]
    longing to hear a word for every day,
    joy will break forth within you as you listen for what I'll say.
[35]For the fountain of life pours into you every time that you find me,
    and this is the secret of growing in the delight
    and the favor of the Lord.
[36]But those who stumble and miss me will be sorry they did!
    For ignoring what I have to say will bring harm to your own soul.
    Those who hate me are simply flirting with death!"[b]

Proverbs 9

Wisdom's Feast

[1]Wisdom[c] has built herself a palace[d]
    upon seven pillars to keep it secure.[e]

---

a 8:34 Or "guard the door of my entrances."

b 8:36 To hate wisdom is not only a sign of stupidity, it is a mark of depravity.

c 9:1 Lady Wisdom is a poetic personification representing Christ, the Wisdom of God (1 Corinthians 1:30). This is a classic form of a synecdoche. The Hebrew word *Chokmah* ("wisdom") can also mean "sacred sense." It is the understanding and insight given only by God.

d 9:1 There is a fascinating word play in the Hebrew text. The verb meaning "to build" and the word translated "son" come from the same root. "Build" is *banah* and "son" is *ben*. The house Wisdom is building is a son. You and I are sons of God who are being built into a spiritual house. There is also a verb in the Hebrew for "hewn" (as in stones). We are living stones raised up to be God's temple. See Psalm 127:1, Hebrews 3:5–6, and Matthew 7:24–27 and 16:18.

e 9:1 The seven pillars of wisdom (plural, "wisdoms") point us to the seven days of creation, the seven spirits of God, and the seven components of heavenly wisdom given in James 3:17–18.

²She has made ready a banquet feast
    and the sacrifice has been killed.ᵃ
    She has mingled her wine, and the table's all set.ᵇ
³She has sent out her maidens,
    crying out from the high place,
    inviting everyone to come
    and eat until they're full.
⁴"Whoever wants to know me and receive my wisdom,
⁵Come and dine at my table and drink of my wine.
⁶Lay aside your simple thoughts and leave your paths behind.
    Agree with my ways, live in my truth,
    and righteousness you will find."
⁷If you try to correct an arrogant cynic,
    expect an angry insult in return.
    And if you try to confront an evil man,
    don't be surprised if all you get is a slap in the face!
⁸So don't even bother to correct a mocker,
    for he'll only hate you for it.
    But go ahead and correct the wise;
    they'll love you even more.ᶜ
⁹Teach a wise man what is right
    and he'll grow even wiser.
    Instruct the lovers of God
    and they'll learn even more.
¹⁰The starting point for acquiring wisdom

---

a 9:2 As translated from the Aramaic. The sacrifice points us to Calvary. Wisdom's pillar is a cross. The Hebrew phrase here literally means "She has prepared her meat."

b 9:2 Wisdom's feast will teach us the ways of God. We feed our hearts on revelation truth that transforms us; then we implement with wise strategies the understanding we have learned at the feasting table.

c 9:8 See Psalm 141:5.

is to be consumed with awe as you worship Jehovah God.
To receive the revelation of the Holy One,[a]
you must come to the one who has living-understanding.
[11]Wisdom will extend your life,
making every year more fruitful than the one before.
[12]So it is to your advantage to be wise.
But to ignore the counsel of wisdom
is to invite trouble into your life.[b]

A Spirit Named Foolish

[13]There is a spirit named Foolish,
who is boisterous and brash;
she's seductive and restless.
[14]And there she sits at the gateway to the high places,
on her throne overlooking the city.
[15]She preaches to all who walk by her
who are clueless as to what is happening:[c]
[16]"Come home with me."
She invites those who are easily led astray, saying,
[17]"Illicit sex is the best sex of all.
Our secret affair will be sweeter than all others."[d]

---

a 9:10 Literally, "holy ones."

b 9:12 The Aramaic adds here: "The liar feeds on the wind and chases fantasies, for he has forsaken what is true to travel in a barren wilderness; forgetting the right paths, he leaves his own vineyard to walk with thirst and gather nothing." The Septuagint adds here: "If you forsake folly you will reign forever. Seek discretion and your understanding will bring you knowledge."

c 9:15 Or "who are walking straight ahead on their path."

d 9:17 The Hebrew phrase here literally means "Stolen waters are sweet, and bread eaten in secret is pleasant." This is an obvious metaphor of finding sexual pleasure with someone other than your spouse and trying to get away with it. Finding pleasure in your relationship with your spouse is like drinking from a pure, clean fountain. But stolen water from someone else's fountain is yielding to foolishness. Adultery is always sin.

¹⁸Little do they know when they answer her call
　　that she dwells among the spirits of the dead,
　　and all her guests soon become citizens of hell!ᵃ

Proverbs 10

¹The wisdom of Solomon:ᵇ
　　When wisdom comes to a son,
　　joy comes to a father.
　　When a son turns from wisdom,
　　a mother grieves.
²Gaining wealth through dishonestyᶜ is no gain at all.
　　But honesty brings you a lasting happiness.ᵈ
³The Lord satisfies the longings of all his lovers,ᵉ
　　but he withholds from the wicked what their souls crave.ᶠ
⁴Slackers will know what it means to be poor,
　　while the hard worker becomes wealthy.
⁵Know the importance of the season you're in
　　and a wise son you will be.

---

a 9:18 Older Aramaic and Septuagint manuscripts add a verse here not found in the Hebrew: "But turn away, linger not in the place or even look at her. Don't drink from a strange fountain. Abstain and drink not from an alien fountain, so that you will enjoy a long life."

b 10:1 The title of this section starting with Proverbs 10 indicates a different form. Solomon's four hundred sayings of wisdom fill this section, going through 22:16. This compilation is an assorted collection of proverbs that is not easily outlined but is profound in its scope.

c 10:2 Or "the treasures of wickedness."

d 10:2 Or "Righteousness (honesty) delivers you from death."

e 10:3 Or "satisfies the souls of the righteous."

f 10:3 The Aramaic is, "the property of the evil he demolishes."

But what a waste when an incompetent son
sleeps through his day of opportunity![a]
[6]The lover of God is enriched beyond belief,
but the evil man only curses his luck.[b]
[7]The reputation of the righteous
becomes a sweet memorial to him,
while the wicked life only leaves a rotten stench.[c]
[8]The heart of the wise will easily accept instruction.
But those who do all the talking
are too busy to listen and learn.
They'll just keep stumbling ahead
into the mess they created.
[9]The one who walks in integrity[d]
will experience a fearless confidence in life,
but the one who is devious
will eventually be exposed.
[10]The troublemaker always has a clever plan
and won't look you in the eye,
but the one who speaks correction honestly
can be trusted to make peace.[e]
[11]The teachings of the lovers of God are like
living truth flowing from the fountain of life,

---

a 10:5 Or "To gather in the summer is to be a wise son, but to sleep through the harvest is a disgrace."

b 10:6 The Hebrew is ambiguous and is literally translated "The mouth of the wicked covers violence."

c 10:7 Some Hebrew manuscripts and the Aramaic read, "The name of the wicked will be extinguished."

d 10:9 Or "innocence." The Aramaic is "He who walks in perfection walks in hope."

e 10:10 As translated from the Septuagint. The Hebrew is "The babbling fool comes to ruin."

but the words of the wicked
hide an ulterior motive.[a]
[12]Hatred keeps old quarrels alive,[b]
but love draws a veil over every insult[c]
and finds a way to make sin disappear.
[13]Words of wisdom flow from the one with true discernment.
But to the heartless, words of wisdom
become like rods beating their backside.
[14]Wise men don't divulge all that they know,
but chattering fools blurt out words
that bring them to the brink of ruin.
[15]A rich man's wealth becomes like a citadel of strength,[d]
but the poverty of the poor leaves their security in shambles.
[16]The lovers of God earn their wages for a life of righteousness,
but the wages of the wicked are squandered on a life of sin.[e]
[17]If you readily receive correction,
you are walking on the path to life.
But if you reject rebuke,
you're guaranteed to go astray.[f]
[18]The one who hides his hatred while pretending to be your friend
is nothing but a liar.
But the one who slanders you behind your back
proves that he's a fool, never to be trusted.
[19]If you keep talking, it won't be long
before you're saying something really wrong.

a 10:11 Or "hide violence."
b 10:12 The Aramaic is "Hatred stirs up judgment."
c 10:12 Love will cover up offenses against us, but never our own offenses.
d 10:15 Or "his fortified city."
e 10:16 Or "their harvest of wickedness."
f 10:17 The Aramaic is even more blunt: "Reject rebuke and you're a moron!"

Prove you're wise from the very start—
just bite your tongue and be strong!
[20]The teachings of the godly ones are like pure silver,
bringing words of redemption to others,[a]
but the heart of the wicked is corrupt.
[21]The lovers of God feed many with their teachings,[b]
but the foolish ones starve themselves
for lack of an understanding heart.
[22]True enrichment comes from the blessing of the Lord,
with rest and contentment[c] in knowing
that it all comes from him.
[23]The fool finds his fun in doing wrong,[d]
but the wise delight in having discernment.
[24]The lawless are haunted by their fears
and what they dread will come upon them,[e]
but the longings of the lovers of God will all be fulfilled.
[25]The wicked are blown away by every stormy wind.
But when a catastrophe comes,
the lovers of God have a secure anchor.
[26]To trust a lazy person to get a job done
will be as irritating as smoke in your eyes—
as enjoyable as a toothache!
[27]Living in the worship and awe of God
will bring you many years of contented living.
So how could the wicked ever expect to have a long, happy life?

---

a 10:20 Or "The tongue of the just is like choice silver." Silver is a metaphor for redemption.

b 10:21 The Aramaic is "The lips of the righteous multiply mercy."

c 10:22 Or "with no labor or sorrow attached."

d 10:23 The word translated "fool" means "moron" in the Aramaic.

e 10:24 This speaks of the consequences of sin. There is a Judge who sees all that we do and will call us to account one day.

[28]Lovers of God have a joyful feast of gladness,
    but the ungodly see their hopes vanish right before their eyes.
[29]The beautiful ways of God are a safe resting place[a]
    for those who have integrity.
    But to those who work wickedness
    the ways of God spell doom.
[30]God's lover can never be greatly shaken.
    But the wicked will never inherit
    the covenant blessings.[b]
[31]The teachings of the righteous are loaded with wisdom,
    but the words of the evil are crooked and perverse.
[32]Words that bring delight pour from the lips of the godly,
    but the words of the wicked are duplicitous.

Proverbs 11

Living in Righteousness

[1]To set high standards for someone else,[c]
    and then not live up to them yourself,
    is something that God truly hates.
    but it pleases him when we apply
    the right standards of measurement.[d]
[2]When you act with presumption,
    convinced that you're right,

---

a 10:29 The Aramaic is "The way of Jehovah is power to the perfect."
b 10:30 Or "land." This is metaphor for all of the covenantal blessings.
c 11:1 The Hebrew phrase here literally means "scales of deception [false balances]."
d 11:1 The Hebrew phrase here literally means "a perfect stone." Stones were used as the legitimate weights of balance. Jesus is the perfect Stone. See Revelation 2:17.

don't be surprised if you fall flat on your face!
But walking in humility helps you to make wise decisions.
[3]Integrity will lead you to success and happiness,
but treachery will destroy your dreams.
[4]When Judgment Day comes,
all the wealth of the world won't help you one bit.
So you'd better be rich in righteousness,
for that's the only thing that can save you in death.
[5]Those with good character walk on a smooth path,
with no detour or deviation.
But the wicked keep falling because of their own wickedness.
[6]Integrity will keep a good man from falling.
But the unbeliever is trapped,
held captive to his sinful desires.
[7]When an evil man dies, all hope is lost,
for his misplaced confidence goes in the coffin
and gets buried along with him.
[8]Lovers of God are snatched away from trouble,
and the wicked show up in their place.[a]
[9]The teachings of hypocrites can destroy you,
but revelation knowledge will rescue the righteous.[b]
[10]The blessing that rests on the righteous
releases strength and favor to the entire city,[c]
but shouts of joy will be heard when the wicked one dies.
[11]The blessing of favor resting upon the righteous
influences a city to lift it higher,[d]
but wicked leaders tear it apart by their words.

---

a 11:8 Haman is a classic example of this principle. See Esther 7:10; 9:24–25.
b 11:9 Or "The righteous will be strengthened."
c 11:10 As translated from the Aramaic and the Septuagint.
d 11:11 Jesus describes the church as a city. See Matthew 5:14.

¹²To quarrel with a neighbor is senseless.ᵃ
    Bite your tongue; be wise and keep quiet!
¹³You can't trust a gossiper with a secret;
    they'll just go blab it all.
    Put your confidence instead in a trusted friend,
    for he will be faithful to keep it in confidence.
¹⁴People lose their way without wise leadership,
    but a nation succeeds and stands in victory
    when it has many good counselors to guide it.
¹⁵The evil man will do harm when confronted by a righteous man,
    because he hates those who await good news.ᵇ
¹⁶A gracious, generous woman
    will be honored with a splendidᶜ reputation,
    but the woman who hates the truth
    lives surrounded with disgraceᵈ and by men
    who are cutthroats, only greedy for money.ᵉ
¹⁷A man of kindness attracts favor,
    while a cruel man attracts nothing but trouble.ᶠ
¹⁸Evil people may get a short-term gain,ᵍ
    but to sow seeds of righteousness
    will bring a true and lasting reward.

---

a 11:12 Or "To disparage your neighbor is being heartless."

b 11:15 As translated from the Aramaic and the Septuagint. There is a vast difference between this and the Hebrew text, which reads, "You'll be ruined if you cosign for a stranger, and a hater of handshakes will be safe."

c 11:16, Or "glorious."

d 11:16 As translated from the older Aramaic and Septuagint texts, but is not included in newer Hebrew manuscripts. There is an additional line added by the Aramaic and the Septuagint: "The lazy will lack, but the diligent support themselves financially."

e 11:16 The Septuagint is "the diligent obtain wealth."

f 11:17 The Hebrew text indicates this trouble could be physical, related to one's health.

g 11:18 Or "wages of deception."

¹⁹A son of righteousness[a] experiences the abundant life,
 but the one who pursues evil hurries to his own death.
²⁰The Lord can't stand the stubborn heart bent toward evil,
 but he treasures those whose ways are pure.[b]
²¹Assault your neighbor and you will certainly be punished,[c]
 but God will rescue the children of the godly.
²²A beautiful woman who abandons good morals
 is like a fine gold ring dangling from a pig's snout.
²³True lovers of God are filled with longings
 for what is pleasing and good,
 but the wicked can only expect doom.
²⁴Generosity brings prosperity,
 but withholding from charity brings poverty.
²⁵Those who live to bless others[d]
 will have blessings heaped upon them,
 and the one who pours out his life to pour out blessings
 will be saturated with favor.
²⁶People will curse the businessman with no ethics,
 but the one with a social conscience receives praise from all.[e]
²⁷Living your life seeking what is good for others brings untold favor,
 but those who wish evil for others
 will find it coming back on them.
²⁸Keep trusting in your riches and down you'll go!
 But the lovers of God rise up like flowers in the spring.
²⁹The fool who brings trouble to his own family

---

a 11:19 As translated from one Hebrew manuscript, the Aramaic, and the Septuagint. Most Hebrew manuscripts have "The one who pursues righteousness."
b 11:20 Or "wholehearted."
c 11:21 As translated from the Aramaic and the Targum (Hebrew-Aramaic commentary).
d 11:25 The Hebrew phrase here literally means "the soul of blessing will grow fat."
e 11:26 The Hebrew phrase here literally means "The one who withholds produce will be cursed, but blessing will be on the head of the one who sells it."

will be cut out of the will,
    and the family servant will do better than he.
30But a life lived loving God bears lasting fruit,
    for the one who is truly wise wins souls.[a]
31If the righteous are barely saved,
    what's in store for all the wicked?[b]

Proverbs 12

It's Right to Live for God

1To learn the truth you must long to be teachable,[c]
    or you can despise correction and remain ignorant.
2If your heart is right, favor flows from the Lord,
    but a devious heart invites His condemnation.
3You can't expect success by doing what's wrong.
    But the lives of his lovers are deeply rooted and firmly planted.
4The integrity and strength of a virtuous wife[d]
    transforms her husband into an honored king.[e]

---

a 11:30 As translated from the Hebrew. The Aramaic and the Septuagint read, "The souls of violent ones will be removed."

b 11:31 As translated from the Septuagint. See also 1 Peter 4:18.

c 12:1 There are times when even the wise need correction, but they will appreciate its value.

d 12:4 There is an amazing Hebrew word used here. It is more commonly used to describe warriors, champions, and mighty ones. Many translations read, "an excellent wife." But the meaning of the Hebrew word *chayil* is better translated "an army that is wealthy, strong, mighty, powerful, with substance, valiant, virtuous, or worthy."

e 12:4 Or "An excellent wife is the crown of her husband." By implication, her dignity makes him a king.

but the wife who disgraces her husband
   weakens the strength of his identity.[a]
5 The lovers of God are filled with good ideas
   that are noble and pure,
   but the schemes of the sinner
   are crammed with nothing but lies.
6 The wicked use their words to ambush and accuse,[b]
   but the lovers of God speak to defend and protect.
7 The wicked are taken out, gone for good,
   but the godly families shall live on.
8 Everyone admires a man of principles,
   but the one with a corrupt heart is despised.
9 Just be who you are and work hard for a living,
   for that's better than pretending to be important
   and starving to death.
10 A good man takes care of the needs of his pets,
   while even the kindest acts of a wicked man are still cruel.
11 Work hard at your job and you'll have what you need.
   Following a get-rich-quick scheme is nothing but a fantasy.
12 The cravings of the wicked are only for what is evil,[c]
   but righteousness is the core motivation for the lovers of God,
   and it keeps them content and flourishing.[d]

Wisdom Means Being Teachable

13 The wicked will get trapped by their words

---

a 12:4 Or "She is like cancer in his bones." Bones are a metaphor for inner strength, our inner being or identity.

b 12:6 Or "lie in wait for blood." This is a figure of speech for accusation.

c 12:12 As translated from the Septuagint. The Hebrew is "Thieves crave the loot of other thieves."

d 12:12 The meaning of the Hebrew text of verse 12 is uncertain.

of gossip, slander, and lies.[a]
But for the righteous, honesty is its own defense.
[14]For there is great satisfaction in speaking the truth,
and hard work brings blessings back to you.
[15]A fool is in love with his own opinion,
but wisdom means being teachable.

Learning to Speak Wisely

[16]If you shrug off an insult and refuse to take offense,
you demonstrate discretion indeed.[b]
But the fool has a short fuse
and will immediately let you know when he's offended.
[17]Truthfulness marks the righteous,
but the habitual liar can never be trusted.
[18]Reckless words are like the thrusts of a sword,
cutting remarks meant to stab and to hurt.[c]
But the words of the wise soothe and heal.
[19]Truthful words will stand the test of time,
but one day every lie will be seen for what it is.
[20]Deception fills the hearts of those who plot harm,
but those who plan for peace[d] are filled with joy.
[21]Calamity is not allowed to overwhelm the righteous,
but there's nothing but trouble waiting for the wicked.
[22]Live in the truth and keep your promises,
and the Lord will keep delighting in you,
but he detests a liar.
[23]Those who possess wisdom don't feel the need

---

a 12:13 The Hebrew is simply, "sinful words," which imply gossip, slander and lies.
b 12:16 Or "A shrewd man conceals his shame."
c 12:18 Implied in the text.
d 12:20 Or "counselors of peace."

to impress others with what they know,
but foolish ones make sure their ignorance is on display.
[24]If you want to reign in life,[a]
don't sit on your hands.
Instead work hard at doing what's right,
for the slacker will end up working
to make someone else succeed.
[25]Anxious fear brings depression,
but a life-giving word of encouragement
can do wonders to restore joy to the heart.[b]
[26]Lovers of God give good advice to their friends,[c]
but the counsel of the wicked will lead them astray.
[27]A passive person won't even complete a project,[d]
but a passionate person makes good use
of his time, wealth, and energy.
[28]Abundant life is discovered by walking in righteousness,
but holding on to your anger leads to death.[e]

---

a 12:24 The Hebrew word for "reign" (*mashal*) is the title of the book—Proverbs. See introduction and the footnote on 1:1.

b 12:25 This insightful proverb can also be translated "Stop worrying! Think instead of what brings you gladness." Our focus must never be on what we can't change but on the everlasting joy we have in Christ. Sometimes we have to find the life-giving word of encouragement rising up in our own hearts. This is the secret of finding perpetual encouragement by the Word that lives in us.

c 12:26 As translated from older Aramaic manuscripts. The Hebrew is uncertain.

d 12:27 Implied in the text, paraphrased from an uncertain Hebrew phrase. An alternate translation would be "A lazy person won't get to roast the game he caught, but the wealth of a diligent person is precious."

e 12:28 As translated from the Septuagint and the Aramaic. The Hebrew is uncertain.

Proverbs 13

Living Wisely

[1] A wise son or daughter desires a father's discipline,
    but the know-it-all never listens to correction.
[2] The words of the wise are kind and easy to swallow,
    but the unbeliever just wants to pick a fight and argue.
[3] Guard your words and you'll guard your life,
    but if you don't control your tongue,
    it will ruin everything.
[4] The slacker wants it all and ends up with nothing,
    but the hard worker ends up with all that he longed for.
[5] Lovers of God hate what is phony and false,
    but the wicked are full of shame and behave shamefully.[a]
[6] Righteousness is like a shield of protection
    guarding those who keep their integrity,
    but sin is the downfall of the wicked.
[7] One pretends to be rich but is poor.
    Another pretends to be poor but is quite rich.[b]
[8] The self-assurance of the rich is their money,[c]
    but people don't kidnap and extort the poor!
[9] The virtues of God's lovers shine brightly in the darkness,
    but the flickering lamp of the ungodly will be extinguished.
[10] Wisdom opens your heart to receive wise counsel,

---

a 13:5 The Hebrew word used here literally means "to cause a stink" or "to emit an odor." This is a figure of speech for what is shameful.

b 13:7 It is never godly to be a phony. It's always better to be who you are and avoid pretense.

c 13:8 The Aramaic is "The salvation of the soul is a man's true wealth."

but pride closes your ears to advice
and gives birth to only quarrels and strife.

[11]Wealth quickly gained is quickly wasted—[a]
easy come, easy go!
But if you gradually gain wealth,
you will watch it grow.

[12]When hope's dream seems to drag on and on,
the delay can be depressing.
But when at last your dream comes true,
life's sweetness will satisfy your soul.[b]

[13]Despise the Word, will you?
Then you'll pay the price and it won't be pretty!
But the one who honors the Father's holy instructions
will be rewarded.

[14]When the lovers of God teach you truth,
a fountain of life opens up within you,
and their wise instruction will deliver you
from the ways of death.

[15]Everyone admires a wise, sensible person,
but the treacherous walk on the path of ruin.[c]

[16]Everything a wise and shrewd man does
comes from a source of revelation-knowledge,[d]
but the behavior of a fool puts foolishness on parade![e]

[17]An undependable messenger causes a lot of trouble,

---

a 13:11 Or "Wealth gained by fraud will dwindle."
b 13:12 Or "It is a tree of life."
c 13:15 As translated from the Aramaic and the Septuagint. The Hebrew is uncertain.
d 13:16 Or "A wise person thinks ahead."
e 13:16 The implication is that the fool is unable to finish anything he begins.

but the trustworthy and wise messengers
release healing wherever they go.[a]

[18]Poverty and disgrace come to the one
who refuses to hear criticism.[b]
But the one who is easy to correct is on the path of honor.

[19]When God fulfills your longings,
sweetness fills your soul.
But the wicked refuse to turn from darkness
to see their desires come to pass.[c]

[20]If you want to grow in wisdom,
then spend time with the wise.
Walk with the wicked
and you'll eventually become just like them.

[21]Calamity chases the sin-chaser,
but prosperity pursues the God-lover.

[22]The benevolent man leaves an inheritance
that endures to his children's children,
but the wealth of the wicked is treasured up for the righteous.

[23]The lovers of God will live a long life and get to enjoy their wealth,
but the ungodly will suddenly perish.[d]

[24]If you withhold correction and punishment[e] from your children,

---

a 13:17 God's sons and daughters are peacemakers, healers, and faithful deliverers for others.

b 13:18 As translated from the Hebrew. The Septuagint is "Instruction removes poverty and disgrace."

c 13:19 Implied by the Hebrew parallelism of the text.

d 13:23 As translated from the Septuagint. The Hebrew is "In the fallow ground of the poor there is abundance of food, but injustice sweeps it away." The Aramaic is "Those who don't find the way of life destroy many years of wealth and some are utterly destroyed." There is a vast difference in the three translations. The translator has chosen to follow the Septuagint.

e 13:24 Or "sparing the rod." Corporal punishment was common in premodern societies.

you demonstrate a lack of true love.
So prove your love and be prompt to punish them.[a]
25The lovers of God will have more than enough,
but the wicked will always lack what they crave.

Proverbs 14

The House of Wisdom

1Every wise woman encourages and builds up her family,
but a foolish woman over time
will tear it down by her own actions.
2Lovers of truth follow the right path
because of their wonderment and worship of God.
But the devious display their disdain for him.
3The words of a proud fool will all come back to haunt him.
But the words of the wise
will become a shield of protection around them.
4The only clean stable is an empty stable.
So if you want the work of an ox and enjoy an abundant harvest,
you'll have a mess or two to clean up!
5An honest witness will never lie,
but a deceitful witness lies with every breath.
6The intellectually arrogant seek for wisdom,
but they never seem to discover
what they claim they're looking for.
For revelation-knowledge flows to the one
who hungers for understanding.

a 13:24 Or "The one who spares the rod hates his child."

[7]The words of the wise are like weapons of knowledge.[a]
     If you need wise counsel, stay away from the fool.
[8]For the wisdom of the wise will keep life on the right track,
     while the fool only deceives himself
     and refuses to face reality.
[9]Fools mock the need for repentance,[b]
     while the favor of God rests upon all his lovers.
[10]Don't expect anyone else to fully understand
     both the bitterness and the joys
     of all you experience in your life.
[11]The household of the wicked is soon torn apart,
     while the family of the righteous flourishes.
[12]You can rationalize it all you want
     and justify the path of error you have chosen,
     but you'll find out in the end
     that you took the road to destruction.
[13]Superficial laughter can hide a heavy heart,
     but when the laughter ends, the pain resurfaces.
[14]Those who turn from the truth get what they deserve,
     but a good person receives a sweet reward.[c]
[15]A gullible person will believe anything,
     but a sensible person will confirm the facts.
[16]A wise person is careful in all things and turns quickly from evil,
     while the impetuous fool moves ahead with overconfidence.

---

a 14:7 As translated from the Aramaic.
b 14:9 Or "Fools mock guilt (or guilt offering)." The Septuagint is "The house of the transgressor owes purification."
c 14:14 As translated from Hebrew manuscripts. The Aramaic is "A good man will be filled from the awe of his soul."

¹⁷An impulsive person has a short fuse and can ruin everything,
  but the wise show self-control.ᵃ
¹⁸The naïve demonstrate a lack of wisdom,
  but the lovers of wisdom are crowned
  with revelation-knowledge.
¹⁹Evil ones will pay tribute to good people
  and eventually come to be servants of the godly.ᵇ
²⁰The poor are disliked even by their neighbors,
  but everyone wants to get close to the wealthy.
²¹It's a sin to despise one who is less fortunate than you,ᶜ
  but when you are kind to the poor,
  you will prosper and be blessed.
²²Haven't you noticed how evil schemers always wander astray?
  But kindness and truth come to those
  who make plans to be pure in all their ways.ᵈ
²³If you work hard at what you do,
  great abundance will come to you.
  But merely talking about getting rich
  while living to only pursue your pleasuresᵉ
  brings you face-to-face with poverty.ᶠ

---

a 14:17 As translated from the Aramaic. The Hebrew is "And a crafty schemer is hated."

b 14:19 Implied in the text. The Hebrew phrase literally means "They will come [or bow] at the gates of the righteous."

c 14:21 Implied in the Hebrew parallelism. The Hebrew phrase here literally means "your neighbor."

d 14:22 Both the Aramaic and the Septuagint insert a verse here that is not found in the Hebrew: "The followers of evil don't understand mercy and faith, but you'll find kindness and faith with those who do good."

e 14:23 As translated from the Septuagint.

f 14:23 There is an additional verse found here in the Aramaic that is missing from the Hebrew text: "The Lord Jehovah heals every sickness, but evil speaking makes you sick [harms you]."

²⁴The true net worth of the wise[a] is the wealth that wisdom imparts.
    But the way of life for the fool is his foolishness.[b]
²⁵Speak the truth and you'll save souls,
    but in the spreading of lies treachery thrives.
²⁶Confidence and strength flood the hearts
    of the lovers of God who live in awe of him,
    and their devotion provides their children
    with a place of shelter and security.[c]
²⁷To worship God in wonder and awe
    opens a fountain of life within you,
    empowering you to escape death's domain.[d]
²⁸A king glories in the number of his loyal followers,
    but a dwindling population spells ruin for any leader.
²⁹When your heart overflows with understanding
    you'll be very slow to get angry.
    But if you have a quick temper,
    your impatience will be quickly seen by all.
³⁰A tender, tranquil heart will make you healthy,[e]
    but jealousy can make you sick.
³¹Insult your Creator, will you?
    That's exactly what you do
    every time that you oppress the powerless![f]
    Showing kindness to the poor is equal to honoring your Maker.
³²The wicked are crushed by every calamity,

---

a 14:24 Or "the crown of the wise."
b 14:24 The Aramaic word translated here as "foolishness" can also mean "insanity."
c 14:26 To live as a passionate lover of God will bring benefit even to your children.
d 14:27 Or "empowering you to turn from the deadly snares."
e 14:30 Or "A heart of healing is the life of the flesh."
f 14:31 Or "slander the poor." Every human being is made in God's image, including the poor.

but the lovers of God find a strong hope
even in the time of death.[a]
33Wisdom soothes the heart of the one with living-understanding,
but the heart of the fool just stockpiles stupidity.
34A nation is exalted by the righteousness of its people,
but sin heaps disgrace upon the land.
35A wise and faithful servant receives promotion from the king,
but the one who acts disgracefully
gets to taste the anger of the king.[b]

Proverbs 15

Wisdom Far Better than Wickedness

1Respond gently when you are confronted
and you'll defuse the rage of another.
Responding with sharp, cutting words[c] will only make it worse.
Don't you know that being angry
can ruin the testimony of even the wisest of men?[d]
2When wisdom speaks, understanding becomes attractive.
But the words of the fool make their ignorance look laughable.[e]
3The eyes of the Lord are everywhere[f]
and he takes note of everything that happens.

---

a 14:32 Our strong hope is that our lives will continue in the presence of God in the resurrection glory. Both the Septuagint and the Aramaic read quite differently: "But the one who trusts in his integrity is righteous."
b 14:35 As translated from the Hebrew. The Septuagint reads, "And by his good behavior shame is removed."
c 15:1 Or "painful words."
d 15:1 This is found only in the Septuagint.
e 15:2 The Aramaic reads, "The mouths of fools vomit a curse."
f 15:3 The eyes of the Lord can also be a metaphor of His prophets.

He watches over his lovers,
and he also sees the wickedness of the wicked.
⁴When you speak healing words,
you offer others fruit from the tree of life.
But unhealthy, negative words do nothing but crush their hopes.ᵃ
⁵You're stupid to mock the instruction of a father,
but welcoming correction will make you brilliant.ᵇ
⁶There is power in the house of the righteous,ᶜ
but the house of the wicked is filled with trouble,
no matter how much money they have.
⁷When wisdom speaks, revelation-knowledge is released,ᵈ
but finding true wisdom in the word of a fool is futile.
⁸It is despicable to the Lord
when people use the worship of the Almighty
as a cloak for their sin,ᵉ
but every prayer of his godly lovers is pleasing to his heart.
⁹The Lord detests the lifestyle of the wicked,
but he loves those who pursue purity.ᶠ
¹⁰Severe punishment awaits the one
who turns away from the truth,
and those who rebel against correction will die.
¹¹Even hell itself holds no secrets from the Lord God,

---

a 15:4 Or "Perverse words are the crushing of the spirit."

b 15:5 The Septuagint adds a verse that is not found in the Hebrew: "In great righteousness there is great strength. But the ungodly will one day perish from the earth."

c 15:6 As translated from the Septuagint and the Aramaic. The Hebrew changes the concept of power to prosperity. Both concepts are valid.

d 15:7 Or "is scattered like seed."

e 15:8 Or "the sacrifice of the wicked"; that is, worshipping God with a wicked heart, only to hide sin. Our yielded heart must be the sacrifice we offer to God.

f 15:9 The Aramaic reads, "He shows mercy to the one who practices righteousness."

for all is exposed before his eyes,
and so much more the heart of every human being.
¹²The know-it-all never esteems the one who tries to correct him.
He refuses to seek good advice from the wise.[a]

Living an Ascended Life

¹³A cheerful heart puts a smile on your face,
but a broken heart leads to depression.
¹⁴Lovers of God[b] hunger after truth,
but those without understanding
feast on foolishness and don't even realize it.
¹⁵Everything seems to go wrong
when you feel weak and depressed.
But when you choose to be cheerful,
every day will bring you more and more joy and fullness.[c]
¹⁶It's much better to live simply,
surrounded in holy awe and worship of God,
than to have great wealth with a home full of trouble.
¹⁷It's much better to have a kind, loving family, even with little,
than to have great wealth
with nothing but hatred and strife all around you.[d]
¹⁸A touchy, hot-tempered man picks a fight,
but the calm, patient man knows how to silence strife.
¹⁹Nothing seems to work right[e] for the lazy man,
but life seems smooth and easy when your heart is virtuous.

---

a 15:12 Another way to say this is "The one who hates authority has no love for being taught."
b 15:14 Or "the upright" (Aramaic).
c 15:15 The Septuagint reads quite differently: "And the good (heart) is always calm."
d 15:17 Or "Better to have a meal of vegetables surrounded with love and grace than a fattened ox where there is hatred."
e 15:19 Or "The way is blocked with thorns."

²⁰When a son learns wisdom,
>   a father's heart is glad.
>   But the man who shames^a his mother is a foolish son.

²¹The senseless fool treats life like a joke,
>   but the one with living-understanding makes good choices.

²²Your plans will fall apart right in front of you
>   if you fail to get good advice.
>   But if you first seek out multiple counselors,
>   you'll watch your plans succeed.

²³Everyone enjoys giving great advice.
>   But how delightful it is to say the right thing at the right time!

²⁴The life path of the prudent lifts them progressively heavenward,
>   delivering them from the death spiral
>   that keeps tugging them downward.

²⁵The Lord champions the widow's cause,^b
>   but watch him as he smashes down the houses of the haughty!

²⁶The Lord detests wicked ways of thinking,^c
>   but he enjoys lovely and delightful words.

²⁷The one who puts earning money above his family
>   will have trouble at home,
>   but those who refuse to exploit others
>   will live in peace.^d

²⁸Lovers of God think before they speak,
>   but the careless blurt out wicked words meant to cause harm.

²⁹The Lord doesn't respond to the wicked,
>   but he's moved to answer the prayers of his godly lovers.

---

a 15:20 Or "despises."
b 15:25 Or "The Lord maintains the boundaries of the widow."
c 15:26 Or "the thoughts of the wicked."
d 15:27 Implied in the text.

³⁰Eyes that focus on what is beautifulᵃ bring joy to the heart,
    and hearing a good report
    refreshes and strengthens the inner being.ᵇ
³¹Accepting constructive criticism
    opens your heart to the path of life,
    making you right at home among the wise.
³²Refusing constructive criticism shows
    you have no interest in improving your life,
    for revelation-insight only comes as you accept correction
    and the wisdom that it brings.
³³The source of revelation-knowledge is found
    as you fall down in surrender before the Lord.
    Don't expect to see Shekinah gloryᶜ
    until the Lord sees your sincere humility.

Proverbs 16

Wisdom Exalts God

¹Go ahead and make all the plans you want,
    but it's the Lord who will ultimately direct your steps.ᵈ
²We are all in love with our own opinions,
    convinced they're correct.

---

a 15:30 As translated from the Septuagint. The Hebrew is "The light of the eyes brings joy."

b 15:30 The Hebrew here literally means "makes fat your bones." Bones picture our inner being.

c 15:33 Or "Before honor is humility." The Hebrew uses the word *kabod,* which is translated as "glory" 156 times in the Old Testament..

d 16:1 As translated from the Septuagint. The Hebrew and Aramaic read, "The Lord gives the right reply."

But the Lord is in the midst of us,[a]
 testing and probing our every motive.
[3]Before you do anything,
 put your trust totally in God and not in yourself.[b]
 Then every plan you make will succeed.
[4]The Lord works everything together to accomplish his purpose.[c]
 Even the wicked are included in his plans—
 he sets them aside for the day of disaster.
[5]Exalting yourself is disgusting to the Lord,
 for pride attracts his punishment—
 and you can count on that!
[6]You can avoid evil through surrendered worship
 and the fear of God,
 for the power of his faithful love
 removes sin's guilt and grip over you.
[7]When the Lord is pleased with the decisions you've made,
 he activates grace to turn enemies into friends.
[8]It is better to have little with a heart that loves justice
 than to be rich and not have God on your side.
[9]Within your heart you can make plans for your future,
 but the Lord chooses the steps you take to get there.

Living like a King

[10]A king speaks the revelation of truth,
 so he must be extraordinarily careful
 in the decrees that he makes.

---

a 16:2 Or "in the midst of spirits."
b 16:3 Or "Commit your business to God."
c 16:4 Or "for its answer."

[11]The Lord expects you to be fair in every business deal,
    for he is the one who sets the standards for righteousness.[a]
[12]Kings and leaders despise wrongdoing,
    for the true authority to rule and reign
    is built on a foundation of righteousness.
[13]Kings and leaders love to hear godly counsel,
    and they love those who tell them the truth.
[14]The anger of a king releases the messenger of death,[b]
    but a wise person will know how to pacify his wrath.
[15]Life-giving light streams from the presence of a king,[c]
    and his favor is showered upon those who please him.
[16]Everyone wants gold, but wisdom's worth[d] is far greater.
    Silver is sought after,
    but a heart of understanding yields a greater return.
[17]Repenting from evil places you on the highway of holiness.
    Protect purity and you protect your life.[e]
[18]Your boast becomes a prophecy of a future failure.
    The higher you lift up yourself in pride,[f]
    the harder you'll fall in disgrace.
[19]It's better to be meek and lowly and live among the poor
    than to live high and mighty among the rich and famous.

---

a 16:11 Or "Honesty with scales and balances is the way of the Lord, for all the stones in the bag are established by Him."

b 16:14 See 1 Kings 2:25, 29–34, 46.

c 16:15 The Septuagint reads, "The king's son is in the light of life."

d 16:16 The Septuagint is, "nests of wisdom."

e 16:17 There are two proverbs inserted here in the Septuagint that are not found in the Hebrew or Aramaic: "Receive instruction and you'll be prosperous; he who listens to correction shall be made wise." "He who guards his ways preserves his own soul; he who loves his life will watch his words."

f 16:18 Or "overconfidence."

²⁰One skilled in business discovers prosperity,
    but the one who trusts in God is blessed beyond belief!

Walking with Wisdom

²¹The one with a wise heart is called "discerning,"
    and speaking sweetly to others
    makes your teaching even more convincing.
²²Wisdom is a deep well of understanding
    opened up within you as a fountain of life for others,
    but it's senseless to try to instruct a fool.
²³Winsome words pour from a heart of wisdom,
    adding value to all you teach.
²⁴Nothing is more appealing
    than speaking beautiful, life-giving words.
    For they release sweetness to our souls
    and inner healing to our spirits.[a]
²⁵Before every person there is a path
    that seems like the right one to take,
    but it leads them straight to hell![b]
²⁶Life motivation comes from the deep longings of the heart,
    and the passion to see them fulfilled urges you onward.[c]
²⁷A wicked scoundrel wants to dig up dirt on others,
    only to spread slander and shred their reputation.
²⁸A twisted person spreads rumors;
    a whispering gossip ruins good friendships.
²⁹A vicious criminal can be persuasive,
    enticing others to join him as partners in crime,
    but he leads them all down a despicable path.

---

a 16:24 Or "healing to the bones." Bones become a metaphor of our inner being.
b 16:25 As translated from the Septuagint. The Hebrew is "the ways of death."
c 16:26 The meaning of the Hebrew in this verse is uncertain.

³⁰It's easy to tell when a wicked man
    is hatching some crooked scheme—
    it's written all over his face.
    His looks betray him as he gives birth to his sin.
³¹Old age with wisdom will crown you with dignity and honor,
    for it takes a lifetime of righteousness to acquire it.ª
³²Do you want to be a mighty warrior?
    It's better to be known as one who is patient and slow to anger.ᵇ
    Do you want to conquer a city?
    Rule over your temper before you attempt to rule a city.ᶜ
³³We may toss the coin and roll the dice,
    but God's will is greater than luck.ᵈ

Proverbs 17

Wisdom's Virtues

¹A simple, humble life with peace and quiet
    is far better than an opulent lifestyle with nothing
    but quarrels and strife at home.
²A wise, intelligent servant will be honored above a shameful son.
    He'll even end up having a portion left to him in his master's will.
³In the same way that gold and silver are refined by fire,
    the Lord purifies your heart by the tests and trials of life.

---

a 16:31 Or "Gray hair is a crown of splendor." In the Hebrew culture the old were
  honored above all, especially if they acquired wisdom. See Leviticus 19:32.

b 16:32 The Septuagint is, "It's better to be forgiving than strong."

c 16:32 Implied in the text.

d 16:33 Or "Into the center the lot is cast and from Jehovah is all its judgment." The
  casting of lots was a common form of divination in the premodern societies.

⁴Those eager to embrace evil listen to slander,
    for a liar loves to listen to lies.
⁵Mock the poor, will you?
    You insult your Creator every time you do!
    If you make fun of others' misfortune,
    you'd better watch out—your punishment is on its way.
⁶Grandparents have the crowning glory of life:
    Grandchildren!
    And it's only proper for children to take pride in their parents.ᵃ
⁷It is not proper for a leader to lie and deceive,
    and don't expect excellent words to be spoken by a fool.ᵇ
⁸Wise instruction is like a costly gem.
    It turns the impossible into success.ᶜ
⁹Love overlooks the mistakes of others,
    but dwelling on the failures of others devastates friendships.
¹⁰One word of correction breaks open a teachable heart,
    but a fool can be corrected a hundred times
    and still not know what hit him.
¹¹Rebellion thrives in an evil man,
    so a messenger of vengeanceᵈ will be sent to punish him.ᵉ
¹²It's safer to meet a grizzly bear robbed of her cubs
    than to confront a reckless fool.

---

a 17:6 Or "fathers." There is an additional verse inserted here that is found in the
   Septuagint: "A whole world of riches belongs to the faithful, but the unfaithful don't get
   even a cent."
b 17:7 Two absurd things are to find a fool in leadership and to have a leader in
   foolishness.
c 17:8 "Instruction" is taken from the Aramaic and the Septuagint. The Hebrew reads,
   "bribe."
d 17:11 Or "merciless angels."
e 17:11 This could mean an evil spirit, or calamities and sorrows.

¹³The one who returns evil for good
   can expect to be treated the same way for the rest of his life.ᵃ
¹⁴Don't be one who is quick to quarrel,
   for an argument is hard to stop,
   and you never know how it will end,
   so don't even start down that road!ᵇ
¹⁵There is nothing God hates more
   than condemning the one who is innocent
   and acquitting the one who is guilty.
¹⁶Why pay tuition to educate a fool?
   For he has no intention of acquiring true wisdom.
¹⁷A dear friend will love you no matter what,
   and a family sticks together through all kinds of trouble.
¹⁸It's stupid to run up bills you'll never be able to pay
   or to cosign for the loan of your friend.
   Save yourself the trouble and don't do either one.ᶜ
¹⁹If you love to argue,
   then you must be in love with sin.
   For the one who loves to boastᵈ is only asking for trouble.
²⁰The one with a perverse heart never has anything good to say,ᵉ
   and the chronic liar tumbles into constant trouble.
²¹Parents of a numskull will have many sorrows,
   for there's nothing about his lifestyle that will make them proud.
²²A joyful, cheerful heart brings healing to both body and soul.

a 17:13 Or "Evil will haunt his house."
b 17:14 The Aramaic for this verse reads, "To shed blood provokes the judgment of a ruler."
c 17:18 Implied by the text.
d 17:19 Or "He who builds a high gate." The gate becomes a picture of the mouth. This is a figure of speech for proud boasting.
e 17:20 Or "can expect calamity."

But the one whose heart is crushed
struggles with sickness and depression.
23When you take a secret bribe,
your actions reveal your true character,
for you pervert the ways of justice.
24Even the face of a wise man shows his intelligence.
But the wandering eyes of a fool
will look for wisdom everywhere
except right in front of his nose.
25A father grieves over the foolishness of his child,
and bitter sorrow fills his mother.
26It's horrible to persecute a holy lover of God
or to strike an honorable man for his integrity!
27Can you bridle your tongue when your heart is under pressure?
That's how you show that you are wise.
An understanding heart keeps you cool, calm, and collected,
no matter what you're facing.
28When even a fool bites his tongue[a]
he's considered wise.
So shut your mouth when you are provoked—
it will make you look smart.

Proverbs 18

Wisdom Gives Life

1An unfriendly person isolates himself

---

a 17:28 The Septuagint is "when an unthinking man asks a question."

and seems to care only about his own issues.
    For his contempt of sound judgment makes him a recluse.[a]
²Senseless people find no pleasure in acquiring true wisdom,
    for all they want to do is impress you with what they know.
³An ungodly man is always cloaked with disgrace,
    as dishonor and shame are his companions.[b]
⁴Words of wisdom[c] are like a fresh, flowing brook—
    like deep waters that spring forth from within,
    bubbling up inside the one with understanding.
⁵It is atrocious when judges show favor to the guilty
    and deprive the innocent of justice.
⁶A senseless man jumps headfirst into an argument;
    he's just asking for a beating for his reckless words.[d]
⁷A fool has a big mouth that only gets him into trouble,
    and he'll pay the price for what he says.
⁸The words of a gossip merely reveal the wounds of his own soul,[e]
    and his slander penetrates into the innermost being.
⁹The one who is too lazy to look for work
    is the same one who wastes his life away.
¹⁰The character of God is a tower of strength,[f]
    for the lovers of God delight to run into his heart
    and be exalted on high.
¹¹The rich, in their conceit, imagine that their wealth

---

a 18:1 There are alternate possible translations of this verse in the Hebrew-Aramaic; for example, "An idle man meditates on his lusts and mocks wise instruction."
b 18:3 Implied in the text.
c 18:4 Or "words that touch the heart."
d 18:6 The Aramaic is "His rash words call for death."
e 18:8 Scholars are somewhat uncertain about an exact translation of this phrase. The Aramaic is "The words of a lazy man lead him to fear and evil."
f 18:10 The Hebrew word *migdal*, translated as "tower of strength," is a homonym that can also be translated "bed of flowers."

is enough to protect them.
It becomes their confidence in a day of trouble.[a]
[12]A man's heart is the proudest when his downfall is nearest,
for he won't see glory until the Lord sees humility.
[13]Listen before you speak,
for to speak before you've heard the facts will bring humiliation.
[14]The will to live sustains you when you're sick,[b]
but depression crushes courage and leaves you unable to cope.
[15]The spiritually hungry are always ready to learn more,
for their hearts are eager to discover new truths.
[16]Would you like to meet a very important person?
Take a generous gift.
It will do wonders to gain entrance into his presence.
[17]There are two sides to every story.
The first one to speak sounds true until you hear the other side
and they set the record straight.[c]
[18]A coin toss[d] resolves a dispute
and can put an argument to rest
between formidable opponents.
[19]It is easier to conquer a strong city
than to win back a friend whom you've offended.
Their walls go up, making it nearly impossible to win them back.[e]
[20]Sharing words of wisdom is satisfying to your inner being.

---

a 18:11 The Aramaic is "The wealth of the rich is a strong city, and its glory casts a broad shadow."
b 18:14 The Septuagint is "A wise servant can calm a man's anger."
c 18:17 The text implies that a legal testimony in a courtroom may seem to be correct until cross-examination begins.
d 18:18 The Hebrew is "casting lots."
e 18:19 Or "A brother supported by a brother is like a high, strong city. They hold each other up like the bars of a fortress."

It encourages you to know
that you've changed someone else's life.[a]
21Your words are so powerful
that they will kill or give life,
and the talkative person will reap the consequences.
22When a man finds a wife,
he has found a treasure!
For she is the gift of God to bring him joy and pleasure.
But the one who divorces a good woman
loses what is good from his house.[b]
To choose an adulteress is both stupid and ungodly.[c]
23The poor plead for help from the rich,
but all they get in return is a harsh response.
24Some friendships don't last for long,[d]
but there is one loving friend who is joined to your heart[e]
closer than any other!

Proverbs 19

Wisdom Exalted

1It's better to be honest, even if it leads to poverty,
than to live as a dishonest fool.

---

a 18:20 Or "A man's belly is filled with the fruits of his mouth, and by the harvest of his lips he will be satisfied."

b 18:22 The reference to divorce is not found in the Hebrew text but is included in both the Aramaic and the Septuagint.

c 18:22 This is not included in the Hebrew or Aramaic, but is found in the Septuagint.

d 18:24 Or "A man with too many friends may be broken to pieces."

e 18:24 The Hebrew word used here can be translated "joined together," "stick close," "to cleave," "to pursue," or "to overtake."

²The best way to live is with revelation-knowledge,
for without it, you'll grow impatient and run right into error.ᵃ
³There are some people who ruin their own lives
and then blame it all on God.
⁴Being wealthy means having lots of "friends,"
but the poor can't keep the ones they have.
⁵Perjury won't go unpunished,
and liars will get all that they deserve.
⁶Everyone wants to be close to the rich and famous,
but a generous person has all the friends he wants!
⁷When a man is poor, even his family has no use for him.
How much more will his "friends" avoid him—
for though he begs for help, they won't respond.ᵇ
⁸Do yourself a favor and love wisdom.
Learn all you can,
then watch your life flourish and prosper!
⁹Tell lies and you're going to get caught,
and the habitual liar is doomed.
¹⁰It doesn't seem right when you see a fool
living in the lap of luxury
or a prideful servant ruling over princes.
¹¹A wise person demonstrates patience,
for mercyᶜ means holding your tongue.
When you are insulted,
be quick to forgive and forget it,
for you are virtuous when you overlook an offense.

---

a 19:2 Or "sin."
b 19:7 The Aramaic and the Septuagint add a sentence not found in the Hebrew: "The one who is malicious with his words is not to be trusted."
c 19:11 The word translated "mercy" ("merciful") here is found only in the Septuagint.

[12]The rage of a king is like the roar of a lion,
  but his sweet favor is like a gentle, refreshing rain.
[13]A rebellious son breaks a father's heart,
  and a nagging wife can drive you crazy!
[14]You can inherit houses and land from your parents,
  but a good[a] wife only comes as a gracious gift from God!
[15]Go ahead—be lazy and passive.
  But you'll go hungry if you live that way.
[16]Honor God's holy instructions
  and life will go well for you.
  But if you despise his ways and choose your own plans,
  you will die.
[17]Every time you give to the poor you make a loan to the Lord.
  Don't worry—you'll be repaid in full
  for all the good you've done.
[18]Don't be afraid to discipline your children
  while they're still young enough to learn.
  Don't indulge your children or be swayed by their protests.
[19]A hot-tempered man has to pay the price for his anger.[b]
  If you bail him out once,
  you'll do it a dozen times.
[20]Listen well to wise counsel
  and be willing to learn from correction
  so that by the end of your life
  you'll be known for your wisdom.
[21]A person may have many ideas concerning God's plan for his life,
  but only the designs of his purpose will succeed in the end.

---

a 19:14 Literally, "prudent" or "understanding" wife.
b 19:19 There is an implication in the Hebrew that he will get into legal trouble. An
  alternate translation of this verse could be "An evil-minded man will be injured; if you
  rescue him, his anger will only intensify."

²²A man is charming when he displays tender mercies to others.
  And a lover of God who is poor and promises nothing
  is better than a rich liar who never keeps his promises.ᵃ
²³When you live a life of abandoned love,
  surrendered before the awe of God,
  here's what you'll experience:
  Abundant life. Continual protection.ᵇ
  And complete satisfaction!
²⁴There are some people who pretend they're hurt—
  deadbeats who won't even work to feed themselves.ᶜ
²⁵If you punish the insolent who don't know any better,
  They will learn not to mock.
  But if you correct a wise man,
  he will grow even wiser.
²⁶Children who mistreat their parents
  are an embarrassment to their family and a public disgrace.
²⁷So listen, my child.
  Don't reject correction
  or you will certainly wander from the ways of truth.ᵈ
²⁸A corrupt witness makes a mockery of justice,
  for the wicked never play by the rules.ᵉ
²⁹Judgment is waiting for those who mock the truth,
  and foolish living invites a beating.

---

a 19:22 Implied in the text.
b 19:23 Or "You will not be remembered for evil."
c 19:24 Or "The lazy man buries his fork in his plate and won't even lift it to his mouth."
d 19:27 Or "Stop listening to instruction that contradicts what you know is truth."
e 19:28 Or "The heart of the wicked feeds on evil."

Proverbs 20

Are You Living Wisely?

[1]A drunkard is obnoxious, loud, and argumentative;
    you're a fool to get intoxicated with strong drink.
[2]The rage of a king is like the roar of a lion.
    do you really want to go and make him angry?
[3]A person of honor[a] will put an argument to rest.
    Only the stupid want to pick a fight.
[4]If you're too lazy to plant seed,
    it's too bad when you have no harvest on which to feed.[b]
[5]A man of deep understanding will give good advice,
    drawing it out from the well within.
[6]Many will tell you they're your loyal friends,
    but who can find one who is truly trustworthy?[c]
[7]The lovers of God will walk in integrity,
    and their children are fortunate
    to have godly parents as their examples.
[8]A righteous king sits on his judgment seat
    He scatters evil away from his kingdom
    by his wise discernment.
[9]Which one of us can truly say,

---

a 20:3 Or "it is the glory of a man." It's better to keep a friend than to win a fight.
b 20:4 The Aramaic and the Septuagint read, "Rebuke a lazy man and he still has no shame, yet watch him go beg at harvest time."
c 20:6 Or "A compassionate man is hard to find, but it's even harder to find one who is faithful."

"I am free from sin in my life,
for my heart is clean and pure"?[a]

¹⁰Mark it down:
God hates it when you demonstrate a double standard:
One for "them" and one for "you."

¹¹Every child shows what they're really like by how they act—
you can discern their character,
whether they are pure or perverse.

¹²Lovers of God have been given eyes to see
with spiritual discernment
and ears to hear from God.

¹³If you spend all your time sleeping, you'll grow poor.[b]
So wake up, sleepyhead! Don't sleep on the job.
And then there will be plenty of food on your table.

¹⁴The buyer says, as he haggles over the price,
"That's junk. It's worthless!"
Then he goes out and brags,
"Look at the great bargain I got!"

¹⁵You may have an abundance of wealth,
piles of gold and jewels,
but there is something of far greater worth:
Speaking revelation words of knowledge.

¹⁶Anyone stupid enough to guarantee a loan for a stranger[c]
deserves to have his property held as security.

_a 20:9 The Hebrew word translated "clean" can also mean "perfect" or "holy." The word translated "pure" can also mean "clear, bright, shining, unmixed." Through God's grace, by the blood of Jesus, believers have been purified, made holy, and set free from our sins.

_b 20:13 The Septuagint reads, "Don't love speaking evil."

_c 20:16 Some manuscripts have "a promiscuous woman."

¹⁷What you obtain dishonestly may seem sweet at first,
    but sooner or later you'll live to regret it.[a]
¹⁸If you solicit good advice, then your plans will succeed.
    So don't charge into battle without wisdom,
    for wars are won by skillful strategy.
¹⁹A blabbermouth will reveal your secrets,
    so stay away from people who can't keep their mouths shut.[b]
²⁰If you despise your father or mother,
    your life will flicker out like a lamp,
    extinguished into the deepest darkness.
²¹If an inheritance is gained too early in life,
    it will not be blessed in the end.
²²Don't ever say, "I'm going to get even with them
    if it's the last thing I do!"
    Wrap God's grace around your heart
    and he will be the one to vindicate you.
²³The Lord hates double standards—
    that's hypocrisy at its worst![c]
²⁴It is the Lord who directs your life,
    for each step you take is ordained by God
    to bring you closer to your destiny.
    So much of your life, then, remains a mystery![d]
²⁵Be careful in making a rash promise before God,
    or you may be trapped by your vow and live to regret it.

---

a 20:17 Or "The bread of falsehood may taste sweet at first, but afterward you'll have a
    mouth full of gravel."
b 20:19 The Aramaic adds a line: "One who is faithful in spirit hides a matter."
c 20:23 Or "The Lord hates differing weights, and dishonest scales are wicked."
d 20:24 The Aramaic reads, "So what man is capable of ordering his way?"

²⁶A wise king is able to discern corruption
    and remove wickedness from his kingdom.ᵃ
²⁷The spirit God breathed into manᵇ is like a living lamp,
    a shining light—
    searching into the innermost chamber of our being.
²⁸Good leadershipᶜ is built on love and truth,
    for kindness and integrity
    are what keep leaders in their position of trust.
²⁹We admire the young for their strength and beauty,
    but the dignity of the old is their wisdom.ᵈ
³⁰When you are punished severely, you learn your lesson well—
    for painful experiences do wonders to change your life.

Proverbs 21

God Is the Source of Wisdom

¹It's as easy for God to steer a king's heartᵉ for his purposes
    as it is for him to direct the course of a stream.ᶠ
²You may think you're right all the time,
    but God thoroughly examines our motives.
³It pleases God more when we demonstrate godliness and justice
    than when we merely offer him a sacrifice.

---

a 20:26 Or "A wise king winnows the wicked and turns his chariot wheel over them."
b 20:27 Implied by the Hebrew word *nishmat,* used in Genesis 2:7.
c 20:28 Or "a king's throne."
d 20:29 Or "their gray hair."
e 21:1 Don't forget, we have been made kings and priests by the blood of the Lamb. See
    1 Peter 2:9 and Revelation 1:6 and 5:10.
f 21:1 Because a leader's decisions affect so many people, God will intervene and steer
    them as a farmer steers the course of a stream to irrigate his fields.

⁴Arrogance, superiority, and pride are the fruits of wickedness[a]
    and the true definition of sin.
⁵Brilliant ideas pay off and bring you prosperity,
    but making hasty, impatient decisions
    will only lead to financial loss.[b]
⁶You can make a fortune dishonestly,
    but your crime will hold you in the snares of death![c]
⁷Violent rebels don't have a chance,
    for their rejection of truth and their love of evil
    will drag them deeper into darkness.
⁸You can discern that a person is guilty by his devious actions
    and the innocence of a person by his honest, sincere ways.
⁹It's better to live all alone in a rickety shack
    than to share a castle with a crabby spouse![d]
¹⁰The wicked always crave what is evil;
    they'll show no mercy and get no mercy.[e]
¹¹Senseless people learn their lessons the hard way,
    but the wise are teachable.
¹²A godly, righteous person[f] has the ability

---

a 21:4 Or "the tillage of the wicked." The Aramaic and the Septuagint has "the lamp of the wicked."

b 21:5 The Aramaic is "The thoughts of the chosen one are trusting, but those of the evil one lead to poverty." This verse is missing from the Septuagint.

c 21:6 As translated from the Aramaic and the Septuagint. The Hebrew is "The money will vanish into thin air."

d 21:9 The Septuagint reads, "It's better to live in the corner of an attic than in a large home plastered with unrighteousness."

e 21:10 The Hebrew is "They show no mercy," while the Septuagint reads, "They'll receive no mercy." The translator has chosen to merge both concepts.

f 21:12 The Hebrew is "a righteous one," which can also speak of God, "the Righteous One."

to bring the light of instruction to the wicked
Even though he despises what the wicked do.[a]
13If you close your heart to the cries of the poor,
then I'll close my ears when you cry out to me!
14Try giving a secret gift to the one who is angry with you
and watch his anger disappear.
A kind, generous gift goes a long way
to soothe the anger of one who is livid.[b]
15When justice is served,
the lovers of God celebrate and rejoice,
but the wicked begin to panic.
16When you forsake the ways of wisdom,
you will wander into the realm of dark spirits.[c]
17To love pleasure for pleasure's sake
will introduce you to poverty.
Indulging in a life of luxury[d]
will never make you wealthy.
18The wicked bring on themselves
the very suffering they planned for others,
for their treachery comes back to haunt them.[e]
19It's better to live in a hut in the wilderness
than with a crabby, scolding spouse!

---

a 21:12 As translated from the Septuagint. There are many examples of this in the Bible: Daniel in Babylon, Joseph in Egypt, and the follower of Jesus today who is living among unbelievers.

b 21:14 The Aramaic and Septuagint translate this: "He who withholds a gift arouses anger."

c 21:16 Or "the congregation of the Rephaim." The Rephaim were a pagan tribe of giants and have been equated with spirits of darkness. See Genesis 14:5 and Deuteronomy 2:11.

d 21:17 Or "the lover of wine and oil."

e 21:18 Or "The evil become the ransom payment for the righteous and the faithless for the upright."

²⁰In wisdom's house you'll find delightful treasures
and the oil of the Holy Spirit.ᵃ
But the stupidᵇ squander what they've been given.
²¹The lovers of God who chase after righteousness
will find all their dreams come true:
An abundant life drenched with favor,
and a fountain that overflows with satisfaction.ᶜ
²²A warrior filled with wisdom ascends into the high place
and releases regional breakthrough,
bringing down the strongholds of the mighty.ᵈ
²³Watch your words and be careful what you say,
and you'll be surprised how few troubles you'll have.
²⁴An arrogant man is inflated with pride—
nothing but a snooty scoffer in love with his own opinion.
"Mr. Mocker" is his name!ᵉ
²⁵⁻²⁶Taking the easy way out is the habit of a lazy man,
and it will be his downfall.
All day long he thinks about all the things that he craves,
for he hasn't learned the secret
that the generous man has learned:
Extravagant giving never leads to poverty.ᶠ
²⁷To bring an offering to God with an ulterior motive is detestable,
for it amounts to nothing but hypocrisy.

---

a 21:20 The Hebrew word for "oil" is an emblem of the Holy Spirit.
b 21:20 Or "a fool of a man."
c 21:21 Or "righteousness."
d 21:22 Or "demolishing their strength of confidence."
e 21:24 The Septuagint adds a line: "He who holds a grudge is a sinner."
f 21:25–26 This is implied in the context and is necessary to complete the meaning of
the proverb. The last line of this verse reads in the Septuagint, "The righteous lavish on
others mercy and compassion."

²⁸No one believes a notorious liar,
    but the guarded words of an honest man stand the test of time.
²⁹The wicked are shameless and stubborn,
    but the lovers of God have a holy confidence.
³⁰All your brilliant wisdom and clever insight
    will be of no help at all if the Lord is against you.
³¹You can do your best to prepare for the battle,[a]
    but ultimate victory comes from the Lord God.

Proverbs 22

How to Live a Life of Wisdom

¹A beautiful reputation[b] is more to be desired than great riches,
    and to be esteemed by others is more honorable
    than to own immense investments.[c]
²The rich and the poor have one thing in common:
    The Lord God created each one.
³A prudent person with insight foresees danger coming
    and prepares himself for it.[d]
    But the senseless rush blindly forward
    and suffer the consequences.
⁴Laying your life down in tender surrender before the Lord
    will bring life, prosperity, and honor as your reward.

---

a 21:31 Or "The horse is prepared for the battle."
b 22:1 The Hebrew is simply "name preferred to wealth." The Aramaic indicates it could
    be "the Name [of God]."
c 22:1 Or "silver and gold." Remember, it is Solomon, one of the richest men to ever live,
    who penned these words.
d 22:3 Wise people solve problems before they happen.

[5]Twisted and perverse lives are surrounded by demonic influence.[a]
>If you value your soul, stay far away from them.
[6]Dedicate your children to God
>and point them in the way that they should go,[b]
>and the values they've learned from you
>will be with them for life.
[7]If you borrow money with interest,
>you'll end up serving the interests of your creditors,[c]
>for the rich rule over the poor.
[8]Sin is a seed that brings a harvest;
>you'll reap a heap of trouble with every seed you plant.
>for your investment in sins pays a full return—
>the full punishment you deserve![d]
[9]When you are generous[e] to the poor,
>you are enriched with blessings in return.
[10]Say goodbye to a troublemaker and you'll say goodbye
>to quarrels, strife, tension, and arguments,
>for a troublemaker traffics in shame.[f]
[11]The Lord loves those whose hearts are holy,
>and he is the friend of those whose ways are pure.[g]

---

a 22:5 Or "thorns and snares." This becomes a metaphor of demonic curses and troubles. Thorns are associated with the fall of Adam. Jesus wore a crown of thorns and took away our curse. The snares picture the temptations of evil that the Devil places in our path.

b 22:6 Or "Train them in the direction they are best suited to go." Some Jewish scholars teach this means understanding your children's talents and then seeing that they go into that field.

c 22:7 The Septuagint reads, "The servant will lend to his own master."

d 22:8 As translated from the Septuagint.

e 22:9 The Hebrew word translated as "generous" here actually means "to have a bountiful eye." It is a figure of speech for generosity, a life of helping others.

f 22:10 As translated from the Aramaic.

g 22:11 As translated from the Septuagint. Followers of Jesus enjoy a relationship with our holy King as we live in the light and love to please him.

¹²God passionately watches[a] over
  his deep reservoir[b] of revelation-knowledge,
  but he subverts the lies of those who pervert the truth.
¹³A slacker always has an excuse for not working—
  like, "I can't go to work. There's a lion outside!
  And murderers too!"[c]
¹⁴Sex with an adulteress is like falling into the abyss.
  Those under God's curse jump right in to their own destruction.
¹⁵Although rebellion is woven into a young man's heart,[d]
  tough discipline can make him into a man.
¹⁶There are two kinds of people headed toward poverty:
  Those who exploit the poor
  and those who bribe the rich.[e]

Sayings of the Wise Sages

¹⁷Listen carefully and open your heart.[f]
  Drink in the wise revelation that I impart.
¹⁸You'll become winsome and wise
  when you treasure the beauty of my words.
  And always be prepared to share them at the appropriate time.
¹⁹For I'm releasing these words to you this day,
  yes, even to you, so that your living hope

---

a 22:12 Or "the eyes of the Lord." In the church today, prophets become eyes in the body of Christ. They see and reveal God's heart for his people.

b 22:12 Although the concept of a reservoir is not found in the Hebrew, it is added by the translator for poetic nuance.

c 22:13 This humorous verse uses both satire and a metaphor. There's always an excuse for not working hard. The Aramaic text adds, "and a murderer too!"

d 22:15 The Aramaic word used here means "senseless."

e 22:16 The Hebrew is literally "Oppressing the poor is gain; giving to the rich is loss. Both end up only in poverty."

f 22:17 From this verse to 24:22 we have a collection of proverbs that lead to virtue. They are especially designed for the young person about to enter a career and start a family.

will be found in God alone,
for he is the only one who is always true.
20-21Pay attention to these excellent sayings of three-fold things.[a]
For within my words you will discover
true and reliable revelation.
They will give you serenity[b] so that you can reveal
the truth of the word of the one who sends you.
22Never oppress the poor
or pass laws with the motive of crushing the weak.
23For the Lord will rise to plead their case
and humiliate the one who humiliates the poor.[c]
24-25Walk away from an angry man
or you'll embrace a snare in your soul[d]
by becoming bad-tempered just like him.
26Why would you ever guarantee a loan for someone else
or promise to be responsible for his debts?
27For if you fail to pay you could lose your shirt![e]

---

a 22:20–21 As translated from the Aramaic. Most translators find this verse difficult to convey. The Hebrew can be "I have written excellent things," "I have written three times," "I write thirty sayings (proverbs)," "I have written you previously," or "I have written you generals." The Septuagint reads, "You should copy these things three times." If the Proverbs contain keys to understanding riddles and mysteries (Proverbs 1:2–6), then we have one of those keys given to us here. God speaks in threes, for he is a triune God. We have a body, soul, and spirit. God lived in a three-room house (outer court, holy place, and the chamber of the Holy of Holies). These three-fold dimensions are throughout the Bible.
b 22:20–21 Serenity is only found in the Aramaic.
c 22:23 As translated from the Aramaic. The Hebrew is "He will rob the soul of the one who robs the poor."
d 22:24–25 As translated from the Aramaic.
e 22:27 Or "bed."

²⁸The previous generation has set boundaries in place.
    Don't you dare move them just to benefit yourself.ᵃ
²⁹If you are uniquely gifted in your work,
    you will rise and be promoted.
    You won't be held back—
    you'll stand before kings!

Proverbs 23

Wisdom Will Protect You

¹When you've been invited to dine with a very important leader,
    consider your manners and keep in mind who you're with.
²Be careful to curb your appetite and catch yourself
    before you fall into the trap of wanting all you see.ᵇ
³Don't crave their delicacies,
    for they may have another motive in having you sit at their table.
⁴Don't compare yourself to the rich.ᶜ
    Surrender your selfish ambition and evaluate them properly.
⁵For no sooner do you start counting your wealth
    than it sprouts wings and flies away like an eagle in the sky—
    here today, gone tomorrow!

---

a 22:28 This refers to moving property lines of your neighbors to take more land, or it
    could mean moving landmarks and memorials placed there by ancestors. It also speaks
    to the moral boundaries that the previous generation modeled—they are to be upheld.
b 23:2 Or "put a knife to your throat." When you spend time with an important person,
    think about his needs, not your own, and favor will come on your life.
c 23:4 As translated from the Septuagint.

⁶Be sensible when you dine with a stingy man[a]
  and don't eat more than you should.[b]
⁷For as he thinks within himself, so is he.[c]
    He will grudgingly say, "Go ahead and eat all you want,"
    but in his heart he resents the fact
    that he has to pay for your meal.
⁸You'll be sorry you ate anything at all,[d]
    and all your compliments will be wasted.
⁹A rebellious fool will despise your wise advice,
    so don't even waste your time—save your breath!
¹⁰Never move a long-standing boundary line
    or attempt to take land that belongs to the fatherless.
¹¹For they have a mighty protector,
    a loving redeemer,[e] who watches over them,
    and he will stand up for their cause.
¹²Pay close attention to the teaching that corrects you,
    and open your heart to every word of instruction.
¹³Don't withhold appropriate discipline from your child.
    Go ahead and punish him when he needs it.[f]
    Don't worry—it won't kill him!
¹⁴A good spanking could be the very thing
    that teaches him a lifelong lesson![g]

---

a 23:6 The Hebrew here literally means "an evil eye," which is a metaphor for a stingy man.

b 23:6 Or "Don't crave his delicacies."

c 23:7 The Aramaic, the LXX, and a few Hebrew manuscripts read: "Eating with him is like eating with someone with a hair in his throat—his mind is not with you!"

d 23:8 Or "You'll vomit up the little you've eaten."

e 23:11 The Hebrew word here is goel, which means "kinsman-redeemer." The Aramaic word means "Savior." This shows powerfully how God will take up the grievances of the oppressed.

f 23:13 The Hebrew is "strike them with the rod."

g 23:14 Or "rescues him from death." The Hebrew word is Sheol.

¹⁵My beloved child, when your heart is full of wisdom,
    my heart is full of gladness.
¹⁶And when you speak anointed words,[a]
    we are speaking mouth to mouth![b]
¹⁷Don't allow the actions of evil men
    cause you to burn with anger.[c]
    Instead, burn with unrelenting passion
    as you worship God in holy awe.
¹⁸Your future is bright and filled with a living hope
    that will never fade away.
¹⁹As you listen to me, my beloved child,
    you will grow in wisdom and your heart
    will be drawn into understanding,
    which will empower you to make right decisions.[d]
²⁰Don't live in the excesses of drunkenness or gluttony,
    or waste your life away by partying all the time,[e]
²¹Because drunkards and gluttons sleep their lives away
    and end up broke!
²²Give respect to your father and mother,
    for without them you wouldn't even be here.
    And don't neglect them when they grow old.

---

a 23:16 Or "speak what is right."

b 23:16 This is taken from the Septuagint, and it literally means, "Your lips shall speak with my lips." The Hebrew is "My kidneys (soul) will rejoice." See Numbers 12:6–8, which reveals that God spoke with Moses mouth to mouth (literal Hebrew).

c 23:17 The Hebrew word used here describes an emotion of intense passion. Many translate it "envy" ("Do not envy the sinner"), but that does not describe it fully. Another possible translation would be "zeal."

d 23:19 The Aramaic is "Set up my doctrines in your heart."

e 23:20 Translated from the Aramaic and the Septuagint.

²³Embrace the truth[a] and hold it close.
    Don't let go of wisdom, instruction,
    and life-giving understanding.
²⁴When a father observes his child living in godliness,
    he is ecstatic with joy—nothing makes him prouder!
²⁵So may your father's heart burst with joy
    and your mother's soul be filled with gladness because of you.
²⁶My son, give me your heart
    and embrace fully what I'm about to tell you.
²⁷Stay far away from prostitutes
    and you'll stay far away from the pit of destruction.
    For sleeping with a promiscuous woman is like falling into a trap
    that you'll never be able to escape!
²⁸Like a robber hiding in the shadows
    she's waiting to claim another victim—
    another husband unfaithful to his wife.
²⁹Who has anguish? Who has bitter sorrow?
    Who constantly complains and argues?
    Who stumbles and falls and hurts himself?
    Who's the one with bloodshot eyes?
³⁰It's the one who drinks too much
    and is always looking for a brew.
    Make sure it's never you!
³¹And don't be drunk with wine[b]

---

a 23:23 The Hebrew word here literally means "create the truth" or "give birth to truth" or "possess the truth." This Hebrew word is also used for God as the Creator. See Genesis 14:19 and 22.

b 23:31 As translated from the Septuagint.

but be known as one who enjoys the company
of the lovers of God,[a]
32For drunkenness brings the sting of a serpent,
like the fangs of a viper[b] spreading poison into your soul.
33It will make you hallucinate, mumble,
and speak words that are perverse.
34You'll be like a seasick sailor being tossed to and fro,
dizzy and out of your mind.
35You'll awake only to say, "What hit me?
I feel like I've been run over by a truck!"
Yet off you'll go, looking for another drink!

Proverbs 24

Wisdom's Warning

1Don't envy the wealth of the wicked or crave their company.
2For they're obsessed with causing trouble
and their conversations are corrupt.
3Wise people are builders—[c]
they build families, businesses, communities.
And through intelligence and insight
their enterprises are established and endure.

---

a 23:31 As translated from the Septuagint and a marginal reading of the Hebrew. The
Aramaic is "Meditate on righteousness." The Septuagint adds a line not found in
Hebrew or Aramaic that describes the unflattering life of a drunk: "You will walk around
naked as a pestle!"

b 23:32 Or "horned serpent," or "dragon." This is the Hebrew word *basilisk*, which
comes from a root word meaning "little king." It becomes an emblem of the poison of
demonic power that can cause addictions and rule over the soul like a "little king."

c 24:3 Or "A house is built by wisdom." The house is more than a structure with roof and
a floor. It becomes a metaphor of families, churches, businesses, and enterprises.

4Because of their skilled leadership
the hearts[a] of people are filled with the treasures of wisdom
and the pleasures of spiritual wealth.
5Wisdom can make anyone into a mighty warrior,[b]
and revelation-knowledge increases strength.
6Wise strategy is necessary to wage war,
and with many astute advisers
you'll see the path to victory more clearly.
7Wisdom is a treasure too lofty[c] for a quarreling fool—
he'll have nothing to say when leaders gather together.
8There is one who makes plans to do evil—
"Master Schemer" is his name.
9If you plan to do evil, it's as wrong as doing it.
And everyone detests a troublemaker.
10If you faint when under pressure,
you have need of courage.[d]
11Go and rescue the perishing! Be their savior!
Why would you stand back and watch them
stagger to their death?
12And why would you say, "But it's none of my business"?
The one who knows you completely
and judges your every motive
is also the keeper of souls—and not just yours!

---

a 24:4 Or "inner chambers."
b 24:5 Or "Wisdom makes anyone into a hero." The Aramaic and the Septuagint read,
"It's better to be wise than to be strong."
c 24:7 The Hebrew is actually "Wisdom is coral to a fool." That is, it is unattainable, deep
and hidden.
d 24:10 Or "Your strength is limited." Our weakness often becomes an excuse to quit, but
strength and courage come as the result of faithfulness under pressure. Some interpret
this to mean "If you fail to help others in their time of need, you will grow too weak to
help yourself."

He sees through your excuses and holds you responsible
for failing to help those whose lives are threatened.
¹³Revelation-knowledge is a delicacy,
sweet like flowing honey that melts in your mouth.
Eat as much of it as you can, my friend!
¹⁴For then you will perceive what is true wisdom,
your future will be bright,[a]
and this hope living within will never disappoint you.
¹⁵Listen up, you wicked, irreverent ones—
don't harass the lovers of God[b]
and don't invade their resting place.
¹⁶For the lovers of God may suffer adversity
and stumble seven times,
but they will continue to rise over and over again.
But the unrighteous are brought down by just one calamity
and will never be able to rise again.[c]
¹⁷Never gloat when your enemy meets disaster
and don't be quick to rejoice if he falls.
¹⁸For the Lord, who sees your heart,
will be displeased with you and will pity your foe.
¹⁹Don't be angrily offended over evildoers or be agitated by them.[d]
²⁰For the wicked have no life and no future—
their light of life will die out.[e]
²¹My child, stand in awe of the Lord Jehovah!
Give counsel to others,
but don't mingle with those who are rebellious.

---

a 24:14 The Septuagint is "Your death will be good."
b 24:15 Or "the righteous."
c 24:16 Implied in the text as it completes the parallelism.
d 24:19 The Septuagint is, "Don't rejoice with those who do evil or be jealous of them."
e 24:20 Not only will they die out, but the implication is they will have no posterity.

²²For sudden destruction will fall upon them
and their lives will be ruined in a moment.
And who knows what retribution they will face![a]

Revelation from the Wise

²³Those enlightened with wisdom have spoken these proverbs:
Judgment must be impartial,
for it is always wrong to be swayed by a person's status.
²⁴If you say to the guilty, "You are innocent,"
the nation will curse you and the people will revile you.
²⁵But when you convict the guilty,
the people will thank you and reward you with favor.
²⁶Speaking honestly is a sign of true friendship.[b]
²⁷Go ahead, build your career and give yourself to your work,
but if you put me first, you'll see your family built up![c]
²⁸Why would you be a false accuser and slander with your words?
²⁹Don't ever spitefully say, "I'll get even with him!
I'll do to him what he did to me!"
³⁰⁻³¹One day I passed by the field of a lazy man
and I noticed the vineyards of a slacker.
I observed nothing but thorns, weeds, and broken down walls.
³²So I considered their lack of wisdom,
and I pondered the lessons I could learn from this:
³³⁻³⁴Professional work habits prevent poverty
from becoming your permanent business partner. And—

---

a 24:22 Verses 21 and 22 are translated from the Aramaic.
b 24:26 The Hebrew is literally, "An honest answer is like a kiss on the lips." In the culture of the day, kissing was a sign of authentic friendship and a mark of relationship, which was often expressed in public among friends.
c 24:27 As translated from the Septuagint.

If you put off until tomorrow the work you could do today,
tomorrow never seems to come.

Proverbs 25

¹Solomon's proverbs published by the scribes of King Hezekiah:
²God conceals the revelation of his Word[a]
    in the hiding place of his glory.[b]
    But the honor of kings[c] is revealed to all
    by how they thoroughly search out
    the deeper meaning of all that God says.
³The heart of a king is full of understanding,
    like the heavens are high and the ocean is deep.
⁴If you burn away the impurities from silver,
    a sterling vessel will emerge from the fire.
⁵And if you purge corruption from the kingdom,
    a king's reign will be established in righteousness.
⁶Don't boast in the presence of a king
    or promote yourself by taking a seat at the head table
    and pretend that you're someone important.
⁷For it is better for the king to say to you,
    "Come, you should sit at the head table,"
    than for him to say in front of everyone,

---

a 25:2 Many translate this "a matter," whereas the Hebrew is *dabar*, which is translated more than eight hundred times in the Old Testament as "word."

b 25:2 There is beautiful poetry in the Hebrew text. The word for "hide" is *cathar* and the word for "word" is *dabar*. The Hebrew is actually "*Kabod* (glory) *cathar* (hidden) *dabar* (word)."

c 25:2 We have been made kings and priests, royal lovers of God, because of God's grace and Christ's redeeming blood. See 1 Peter 2:9 and Revelation 5:8–10.

"Please get up and move—
  you're sitting in the place of the prince."
⁸Don't be hasty to file a lawsuit.
    By starting something you wish you hadn't,
    you could be humiliated when you lose your case.
⁹Don't reveal another person's secret
    just to prove a point in an argument,
    or you could be accused of being a gossip
¹⁰And gain a reputation of being one
    who betrays the confidence of a friend.
¹¹Winsome words spoken at just the right time[a]
    are as appealing as apples gilded in gold
    and surrounded with silver.[b]
¹²To humbly receive wise correction
    adorns your life with beauty[c]
    and makes you a better person.
¹³A reliable, trustworthy messenger
    refreshes the heart of his master,[d]
    like a gentle breeze blowing at harvest time—
    cooling the sweat from his brow.
¹⁴Clouds that carry no water

---

a 25:11 The Aramaic reads, "The one who speaks the Word is an apple of gold in a setting of silver." The Septuagint is "A wise word is like a golden apple in a pendant of rubies."

b 25:11 Each one of God's promises are like apples gilded in gold. When we are full of his Spirit we can speak and prophesy words of encouragement that are spoken at the right time for the blessing of others.

c 25:12 Or "an earring of gold, an ornament of fine gold." An earring pierces the ear and is an emblem of a listening heart.

d 25:13 Or "employer."

and a wind that brings no refreshing rain—[a]
that's what you're like when you boast
of a gift that you don't have.[b]

Wisdom Practices Self-control

[15]Use patience and kindness when you want to persuade leaders
and watch them change their minds right in front of you.
For your gentle wisdom will quell the strongest resistance.[c]
[16]When you discover something sweet,
don't overindulge and eat more than you need,
for excess in anything can make you sick of even a good thing.
[17]Don't wear out your welcome
by staying too long at the home of your friends,
or they may get fed up with always having you there
and wish you hadn't come.
[18]Lying about and slandering people
are as bad as hitting them with a club,
or wounding them with an arrow,
or stabbing them with a sword.
[19]You can't depend on an unreliable person
when you really need help.
It can be compared to biting down on an abscessed tooth
or walking with a sprained ankle.

---

a 25:14 The symbols of clouds, wind, and rain are significant. Clouds are often a metaphor for the people of God filled with glory (Hebrews 12:1; Revelation 1:7). Wind is an emblem of the Holy Spirit bringing new life (John 3:6–8). Rain often points to teaching the revelation truths that refresh and water the seeds of spiritual growth (Isaiah 55:8–11). God's anointed people are to be clouds carried by the wind of the Holy Spirit that bring refreshing truths to his people. When we are empty and false, we are clouds without rain. See 2 Peter 2:17 and Jude 1:12.

b 25:14 Or "boast of a promised gift you never intend to give." The Hebrew is literally "to make yourself shine in a gift of falsehood."

c 25:15 Or "Soft words break bones."

²⁰When you sing a song of joy to someone suffering
      in the deepest grief and heartache,
      it can be compared to disrobing in the middle of a blizzard
      or rubbing salt in a wound.
²¹Is your enemy hungry? Buy him lunch.
      Win him over with your kindness.ᵃ
²²Your surprising generosity will awaken his conscienceᵇ
      and God will reward you with favor.
²³As the north wind brings a storm,
      saying things you shouldn'tᶜ brings a storm to any relationship.
²⁴It's better to live all alone in a rundown shack
      than to share a castle with a crabby spouse!ᵈ
²⁵Like a drink of cool water to a weary, thirsty soul,
      so hearing good news revives the spirit.ᵉ
²⁶When a lover of God gives in and compromises with wickedness,
      it can be compared to contaminating a stream with sewage
      or polluting a fountain.
²⁷It's good to eat sweet things,
      but you can take too much.
      It's good to be honored,
      but to seek words of praiseᶠ is not honor at all.
²⁸If you live without restraint
      and are unable to control your temper,

---

a 25:21 Or "Is he thirsty? Give him a drink."
b 25:22 Or "You will heap coals of fire on his head." His heart will be moved and his shame exposed.
c 25:23 Or "words of gossip."
d 25:24 With the exception of one Hebrew letter, this verse is identical to 21:9. See footnote. The Aramaic reads, "than to live with a contentious woman in a house of divisions."
e 25:25 Implied in the text.
f 25:27 This line is translated from the Aramaic.

you're as helpless as a city with broken-down defenses,
open to attack.

Proverbs 26

Don't Be a Fool

¹It is totally out of place to promote and honor a fool,
　　just like it's out of place to have snow in the summer
　　and rain at harvest time.[a]
²An undeserved curse will be powerless to harm you.
　　It may flutter over you like a bird,
　　but it will find no place to land.[b]
³Guide a horse with a whip,
　　direct a donkey with a bridle,
　　and lead a rebellious fool with a beating on his backside!
⁴Don't respond to the words of a fool with more foolish words,
　　or you will become as foolish as he is!
⁵Yet, if you're asked a silly question,
　　answer it with words of wisdom[c]
　　so the fool doesn't think he's so clever.
⁶If you chose a fool to represent you,
　　you're asking for trouble.
　　It will be as bad for you as cutting off your own feet!

---

a 26:1 Both snow and rain are good in their proper season but harmful in the wrong
　　season. So is it harmful to the fool if you affirm him and honor him prematurely.
b 26:2 There is an implication in some Hebrew manuscripts that the curse will go back
　　and land on the one who wrongly spoke it, like a bird going back to its nest.
c 26:5 As translated from the Aramaic.

⁷You can never trust the words of a fool,
 just like a crippled man can't trust his legs to support him.^a
⁸Give honor to a fool and watch it backfire—
 like a stone tied to a slingshot.
⁹The statements of a fool will hurt others^b
 like a thorn bush brandished by a drunk.
¹⁰Like a reckless archer shooting arrows at random
 is the impatient employer
 who hires just any fool who comes along—
 someone's going to get hurt!^c
¹¹Fools are famous for repeating their errors,
 like dogs are known to return to their vomit.
¹²There's only one thing worse than a fool,
 and that's the smug, conceited man
 always in love with his own opinions.

Don't Be Lazy

¹³The lazy loafer says,
 "I can't go out and look for a job—
 there may be a lion out there roaming wild in the streets!"
¹⁴As a door is hinged to the wall,
 so the lazy man keeps turning over, hinged to his bed!
¹⁵There are some people so lazy
 they won't even work to feed themselves.

---

a 26:7 As translated from the Aramaic.
b 26:9 As translated from the Aramaic.
c 26:10 Implied in the context. This is a difficult verse to translate and it reads quite
 differently in the Aramaic and the Septuagint. The Aramaic is "A fool suffers much like
 a drunkard crossing the sea." The Septuagint reads, "Every fool endures much hardship
 and his fury comes to nothing."

¹⁶A self-righteous person^a is convinced he's smarter
   than seven wise counselors who tell him the truth.
¹⁷It's better to grab a mad dog by its ears
   than to meddle and interfere in a quarrel^b
   that's none of your business.

Watch Your Words

^{18–19}The one who is caught lying to his friend
   and says, "I didn't mean it, I was only joking,"
   can be compared to a madman
   randomly shooting off deadly weapons.
²⁰It takes fuel to have a fire—
   a fire dies down when you run out of fuel.
   So quarrels disappear when the gossip ends.
²¹Add fuel to the fire and the blaze goes on.
   So add an argumentative man to the mix
   and you'll keep strife alive.
²²Gossip is so delicious, and how we love to swallow it!
   For slander^c is easily absorbed into our innermost being.
²³Smooth talk^d can hide a corrupt heart
   just like a pretty glaze covers a cheap clay pot.
²⁴Kind words can be a cover to conceal hatred of others,
   for hypocrisy loves to hide behind flattery.
²⁵So don't be drawn in by the hypocrite,
   for his gracious speech is a charade,

---

a 26:16 Or "sluggard." This speaks of a person who lives in fantasy and not reality.
b 26:17 Or "to become furious because of a quarrel that's not yours."
c 26:22 Or "complaining."
d 26:23 As translated from the Septuagint. The Hebrew is "burning words."

nothing but a masquerade
covering his hatred and evil on parade.[a]
[26]Don't worry—he can't keep the mask on for long.
One day his hypocrisy will be exposed before all the world.
[27]Go ahead, set a trap for others—
and then watch as it snaps back on you!
Start a landslide and you'll be the one who gets crushed.
[28]Hatred is the root of slander[b]
and insecurity the root of flattery.[c]

Proverbs 27

Heed Wisdom's Warnings

[1]Never brag about the plans you have for tomorrow,
for you don't have a clue what tomorrow may bring to you.
[2]Let someone else honor you for your accomplishments,
for self-praise is never appropriate.
[3]It's easier to carry a heavy boulder and a ton of sand
than to be provoked by a fool and have to carry that burden!
[4]The rage and anger of others can be overwhelming,
but it's nothing compared to jealousy's fire.
[5]It's better to be corrected openly,
if it stems from hidden love.

---

a 26:25 The Hebrew is "Seven abominations hide in his heart." This is a figure of speech for the fullness of evil, a heart filled to the brim with darkness.
b 26:28 Or "A slanderer hates his victims."
c 26:28 Implied in the text. The Aramaic is "Malicious words work trouble."

⁶You can trust a friend who wounds you with his honesty,[a]
  but your enemy's pretended flattery[b] comes from insincerity.
⁷When your soul is full, you turn down even the sweetest honey.
  But when your soul is starving,
  every bitter thing becomes sweet.[c]
⁸Like a bird that has fallen from its nest
  is the one who is dislodged from his home.[d]
⁹Sweet friendships[e] refresh the soul and awaken our hearts with joy,
  for good friends are like the anointing oil
  that yields the fragrant incense of God's presence.[f]
¹⁰So never give up on a friend or abandon a friend of your father—
  for in the day of your brokenness[g]
  you won't have to run to a relative for help.
  A friend nearby is better than a relative far away.
¹¹My son, when you walk in wisdom,
  my heart is filled with gladness,
  for the way you live is proof
  that I've not taught you in vain.[h]
¹²A wise, shrewd person discerns the danger ahead
  and prepares himself,
  but the naïve simpleton never looks ahead
  and suffers the consequences.

---

a 27:6 Or "Wounds by a loved one are long lasting (effective and faithful)."

b 27:6 Or "kisses."

c 27:7 When we are full of many things and many opinions, the sweet Word of God, like revelation honey, is spurned. Instead, we eat and fill our souls with things that can never satisfy.

d 27:8 Or "banished from his place." As translated from the Aramaic.

e 27:9 Or "counsel."

f 27:9 Implied in the text. The Hebrew text refers to the sacred anointing oil and the incense that burns in the Holy Place.

g 27:10 As translated from the Aramaic.

h 27:11 Implied in the text.

¹³Cosign for one you barely know and you will pay a great price!
Anyone stupid enough to guarantee the loan of another
deserves to have his property seized in payment.
¹⁴Do you think you're blessing your neighbors
when you sing at the top of your lungs early in the morning?
Don't be fooled—
they'll curse you for doing it![a]
¹⁵An endless drip, drip, drip, from a leaky faucet[b]
and the words of a cranky, nagging wife have the same effect.
¹⁶Can you stop the north wind from blowing
or grasp a handful of oil?
That's easier than to stop her from complaining.
¹⁷It takes a grinding wheel to sharpen a blade,
and so a friendly argument can sharpen a man.[c]
¹⁸Tend an orchard and you'll have fruit to eat.
Serve the master's interests
and you'll receive honor that's sweet.
¹⁹Just as no two faces are exactly alike,
so every heart is different.[d]
²⁰Hell and destruction are never filled,
and so the desires of men's hearts are insatiable.
²¹Fire is the way to test the purity of silver and gold,
but the character of a man is tested
by giving him a measure of fame.[e]

---

a 27:14 Or "He who sings in a loud voice early in the morning, thinking he's blessing his
neighbor is no different from he who pronounces a curse."
b 27:15 Or "a constant drip on a rainy day."
c 27:17 Or "a man's face."
d 27:19 As translated from the Aramaic and the Septuagint.
e 27:21 Or "by the things he praises."

[22]You can beat a fool half to death
    and still never beat the foolishness out of him.[a]
[23]A shepherd[b] should pay close attention to the faces of his flock
    and hold close to his heart the condition of those he cares for.
[24]A man's strength, power, and riches[c] will one day fade away,
    not even nations[d] endure forever.
[25–27]Take care of your responsibilities
    and be diligent in your business
    and you will have more than enough—
    an abundance of food, clothing, and plenty for your household.[e]

Proverbs 28

Lovers of God

[1]Guilty criminals experience paranoia
    even though no one threatens them.
    But the innocent lovers of God,
    because of righteousness,
    will have the boldness[f] of a young, ferocious lion!

---

a 27:22 Or "If you pound a fool in a mortar like dried grain with a pestle, still his foolishness will not depart from him."

b 27:23 Implied in the text.

c 27:24 The Hebrew says merely, "riches," while the Aramaic adds, "power (dominion)" and the Septuagint adds, "strength." The translator has chosen to combine them.

d 27:24 Or "a crown (dominion)."

e 27:25–27 An agricultural analogy is used in the Hebrew and Aramaic. The analogy of a farming enterprise has been changed to business here in order to transfer meaning. It is literally, "Gather the hay of the field and hills, and new grass will appear. Lambs will provide clothing, goats will pay for the price of the field, and there will be enough goat's milk for you, your family, and your servant girls."

f 28:1 Or "confidence."

[2]A rebellious nation is thrown into chaos,[a]
    but leaders anointed with wisdom will restore law and order.
[3]When a pauper[b] oppresses the destitute,
    it's like a flash flood that sweeps away their last hope.
[4]Those who turn their backs on what they know is right[c]
    will no longer be able to tell right from wrong.
    But those who love the truth strengthen their souls.[d]
[5]Justice never makes sense to men devoted to darkness,
    but those tenderly devoted to the Lord
    can understand justice perfectly.
[6]It's more respectable to be poor and pure than rich and perverse.
[7]To be obedient to what you've been taught[e]
    proves you're an honorable child,
    but to socialize with the lawless brings shame to your parents.
[8]Go ahead and get rich on the backs of the poor,
    but all the wealth you gather will one day be given
    to those who are kind to the needy.
[9]If you close your heart and refuse to listen to God's instruction,[f]
    even your prayer will be despised.
[10]Those who tempt the lovers of God with an evil scheme
    will fall into their own trap.
    But the innocent who resist temptation will experience reward.
[11]The wealthy in their conceit presume to be wise,
    but a poor person with discernment can see right through them.

---

a 28:2 Or "A rebellious nation will have one leader after another."
b 28:3 This pauper can also be one who is spiritually poor. Some Jewish expositors
    believe it refers to corrupt judges.
c 28:4 The Hebrew word is "the Torah." See also verses 7 and 9.
d 28:4 As translated from the Aramaic. The Septuagint is "build a wall to protect
    themselves."
e 28:7 Or "the Torah."
f 28:9 Or "the Torah."

¹²The triumphant joy of God's lovers releases great glory.ᵃ
But when the wicked rise to power, everyone goes into hiding.ᵇ
¹³If you cover up your sin you'll never do well.
But if you confess your sins and forsake them,
you will be kissed by mercy.
¹⁴Overjoyed is the one who with tender heart trembles before God,
but the stubborn, unyielding heart
will experience even greater evil.
¹⁵Ruthless rulers can only be compared
to raging lions and roaming bears.ᶜ
¹⁶Abusive leaders fail to employ wisdom,
but leaders who despise corruptionᵈ
will enjoy a long and full life.ᵉ
¹⁷A murderer's conscience will torment him—
a fugitive haunted by guilt all the way to the grave
with no one to support him.
¹⁸The pure will be rescued from failure,
but the perverse will suddenly fall into ruin.
¹⁹Work hard and you'll have all you desire,
but chase a fantasyᶠ and you could end up with nothing.
²⁰Life's blessings drench the honest and faithful person,
but punishment rains down upon the greedy and dishonest.
²¹Giving favoritism to the rich and powerful is disgusting,

---

a 28:12 As translated from the Aramaic.
b 28:12 Or "people become victims."
c 28:15 David, before he killed Goliath, went after the lion and the bear. See 1 Samuel 17:34–37. These beasts represented demonic forces of evil over the land. Daniel also mentions the world's ruthless leaders as lions and bears. See Daniel 7:1–8
d 28:16 Or "injustice."
e 28:16 Or "enjoy a long reign."
f 28:19, Or "an empty dream." The Septuagint is "the one who pursues leisure."

and this is the type of judge
who would betray a man for a bribe.[a]
²²A greedy man[b] is in a race to get rich,
but he forgets that he could lose what's most important
and end up with nothing.[c]
²³If you correct someone with constructive criticism,
in the end he will appreciate it more than flattery.
²⁴A person who would reject[d] his own parents and say,
"What's wrong with that?" is as bad as a murderer.
²⁵To make rash, hasty decisions
shows that you are not trusting the Lord.
But when you rely totally on God,
you will still act carefully and prudently.[e]
²⁶Self-confident[f] know-it-alls will prove to be fools.
But when you lean on the wisdom from above,
you will have a way to escape the troubles of your own making.
²⁷You will never go without if you give to the poor.
But if you're heartless, stingy, and selfish,[g]
you invite curses upon yourself.
²⁸When wicked leaders rise to power,

---

a 28:21 As translated from the Aramaic.
b 28:22 Both the Aramaic and Hebrew have "the man with an evil eye." This is a figure of speech for a stingy or greedy man. A person who shuts his heart to the poor is said to have an evil eye. A person with a good eye is someone who looks on the poor with generosity.
c 28:22 As translated from the Aramaic. The Aramaic text sounds very similar to what Jesus says about gaining the world but losing our souls. See Mark 8:36.
d 28:24 As translated from the Septuagint. The Hebrew is "the one who steals from his own parents."
e 28:25 As translated from the Septuagint. The Hebrew is "The greedy person stirs up trouble, but the one who trusts in the Lord will prosper."
f 28:26 Or "those who trust their instincts."
g 28:27 Or "he who hides his eyes from the poor."

good people go into hiding.
But when they fall from power,
the godly take their place.

Proverbs 29

Don't Be Stubborn

¹Stubborn people who repeatedly refuse to accept correction
    will suddenly be broken and never recover.
²Everyone rejoices when the lovers of God flourish,
    but the people groan when the wicked rise to power.
³When you love wisdom, your father is overjoyed.
    But when you associate with prostitutes,
    you waste your wealth in exchange for disgrace.[a]
⁴A godly leader who values justice
    is a great strength and example to the people.
    But the one who sells his influence for money[b]
    tears down what is right.
⁵Flattery can often be used as a trap to hide ulterior motives
    and take advantage of you.
⁶The wicked always have a trap laid for others,
    but the lovers of God escape as they sing and shout
    in joyous triumph!
⁷God's righteous people will pour themselves out for the poor,[c]
    but the ungodly make no attempt
    to understand or help the needy.

---

a 29:3 See Luke 15:11–24.
b 29:4 See 1 Timothy 6:10.
c 29:7 The Hebrew text implies standing up for the legal rights of the poor.

You Can't Argue with a Fool

[8]Arrogant cynics love to pick fights,
     but the humble and wise love to pursue peace.
[9]There's no use arguing with a fool,[a]
     for his ranting and raving prevents you from making a case
     and settling the argument in a calm way.
[10]Violent men hate those with integrity,
     but the lovers of God esteem those who are holy.[b]
[11]You can recognize fools by the way
     they give full vent to their rage
     and let their words fly!
     But the wise bite their tongue and hold back all they could say.
[12]When leaders listen to false accusations,
     their associates become scoundrels.
[13]Poor people and their oppressors
     have only one thing in common—
     God made them both.[c]
[14]The best insurance for a leader's longevity
     is to demonstrate justice for the poor.
[15]Experiencing many corrections and rebukes will make you wise.
     But if left to your own ways,
     you'll bring disgrace to your parents.[d]
[16]When the wicked are in power, lawlessness abounds.
     But the patient lovers of God will one day watch in triumph
     as their stronghold topples!

---

a 29:8 The Hebrew implies an argument in a court of law.
b 29:10 As translated from the Septuagint.
c 29:13 A figure of speech in Hebrew that can literally be translated "God gave them
   both the gift of eyesight." The Septuagint is "The contracts between lenders and
   debtors is observed by the Lord."
d 29:15 As translated from the Septuagint. The Hebrew is "your mother."

¹⁷Correct your child and one day you'll find he has changed
   and will bring you great delight.
¹⁸When there is no clear prophetic vision,[a]
   people quickly wander astray.[b]
   But when you follow the revelation of the Word,[c]
   heaven's bliss fills your soul.
¹⁹A stubborn servant can't be corrected by words alone.
   For even if he understands, he pays no attention to you.
²⁰There's only one kind of person who is worse than a fool:
   The impetuous one who speaks without thinking first.
²¹If you pamper your servants,
   don't be surprised when they expect to be treated as sons.[d]
²²The source of strife is found in an angry heart,
   for sin surrounds the life of a furious man.[e]
²³Lift yourself up with pride and you will soon be brought low,[f]
   but a meek and humble spirit will add to your honor.
²⁴You are your own worst enemy when you partner with a thief,
   for a curse of guilt will come upon you
   when you fail to report a crime.[g]
²⁵Fear and intimidation is a trap that holds you back.

---

a 29:18 The Hebrew word used here can refer to "vision of the night," "dream," "oracle," or "revelation." The Septuagint reads, "Where there is no prophetic seer" or "interpreter."

b 29:18 Or "let loose, stripped, or made naked." The Septuagint reads, "The people become lawless."

c 29:18 Implied in the text. The Hebrew is "Torah."

d 29:21 Or "If you pamper your servant when he is young, he'll become a weakling in the end." The Septuagint reads, "If you live in luxury as a child, you'll become a domestic (servant) and at last will be grieved with yourself." The Aramaic states, "You'll be uprooted in the end."

e 29:22 The Hebrew word translated as "a furious man" can also mean "lord of fury" or "Baal of wrath."

f 29:23 Or "to depression."

g 29:24 Or "when under oath to testify but you do not talk."

But when you place your confidence in the Lord,
   you will be seated in the high place.
²⁶Everyone curries favor with leaders.
   But God is the judge, and justice comes from him.
²⁷The wicked hate those who live a godly life,
   but the righteous hate injustice wherever it's found.

Proverbs 30

The Mysterious Sayings of Agur

¹These are the collected sayings of the prophet Agur, Jakeh's son[a]—
   the amazing revelation[b] he imparted to Ithiel and Ukal.[c]
²God, I'm so weary and worn out,
   I feel more like a beast than a man.
   I was made in your image,[d]
   but I lack understanding.
³I've yet to learn the wisdom

---

a 30:1 This section of Proverbs is attributed to Agur, who gave these oracles to his protégés Ithiel and Ukal. Agur means "to gather a harvest." He was the *son of* Jakeh, which means "blameless" or "obedient." Jakeh could be another name for David, Solomon's father. Many Jewish expositors believe that Agur was a pseudonym for Solomon. Nothing more is mentioned about Agur in the Bible than what we have here, which is typical for other prophets mentioned in the Scriptures. Some believe he could be the "master of the collection of sayings" referred to in Ecclesiastes 12:11. Agur (taken from Agar) means "collector."

b 30:1 Or "mighty prophecy."

c 30:1 The name Ithiel can mean "God is with me" or "God has arrived." This was fulfilled by Christ, for his birth was the advent, the arrival of God to the earth in human form. Ukal means "I am able" or "I am strong and mighty." When placed together, the meaning of these Hebrew names could read, "Gather a harvest of sons who are blameless and obedient. They will have God with them, and they will be strong and mighty." This chapter contains some of the most mystical and mysterious sayings found in Proverbs, with hints of revelation from the book of Job.

d 30:2 Implied in the text, which is extraordinarily difficult to translate with certainty.

that comes from the full and intimate knowledge of you,
the Holy One.

Six Questions

[4]Who is it that travels back and forth
from the heavenly realm to the earth?[a]
Who controls the wind as it blows[b] and holds it in his fists?
Who tucks the rain into the cloak of his clouds?
Who stretches out the skyline from one vista to the other?
What is his name?
And what is the name of his Son?
Who can tell me?

A Pure Heart Is Filled with God's Word

[5]Every promise from the faithful God
is pure and proves to be true.
He is a wrap-around shield of protection for all his lovers
who run to hide in him.
[6]Never add to his words,
or he will have to rebuke you and prove that you're a liar.
[7]God, there are two things I'm asking you for before I die, only two:
[8]Empty out of my heart everything that is false—
every lie, and every crooked thing.
And give me neither undue poverty nor undue wealth—
but rather, feed my soul with the measure of prosperity
that pleases you.
[9]May my satisfaction be found in you.
Don't let me be so rich that I don't need you

---

a 30:4 Jesus solves this riddle in John 3:13. Only Jesus Christ is the master of heavenly
knowledge and wisdom. See also Ephesians 4:7–10.
b 30:4 The Hebrew word *ruach* (wind) is also the term used for the Holy Spirit.

or so poor that I have to resort to dishonesty
just to make ends meet.
Then my life will never detract from bringing glory to your name.
¹⁰Never defame a servant before his master,
for you will be the guilty one
and a curse will come upon you.
¹¹There is a generation rising that curses their fathers
and speaks evil of their mothers.
¹²There is a generation rising that considers themselves
to be pure in their own eyes,ᵃ
yet they are morally filthy,ᵇ unwashed, and unclean.
¹³There is a generation rising that is so filled with pride.
They think they are superior and look down on others.
¹⁴There is a generation rising that uses their words like swords
to cut and slash those who are different.
They would devour the poor, the needy, and the afflicted
from off the face of the earth!
¹⁵There are three words to describe the greedy:
"Give me more!"
There are some things that are never satisfied.
Forever craving more, they're unable to say, "That's enough!"
Here are four:
¹⁶The grave, yawning for another victim,
the barren womb, ever wanting a child,
thirsty soil, ever longing for rain,
and a raging fire, devouring its fuel.
They're all insatiable.

a 30:12 See Judges 21:25.
b 30:12 The Hebrew uses the word excrement.

[17]The eye that mocks his father and dishonors his elderly mother[a]
   deserves to be plucked out by the ravens of the valley
   and fed to the young vultures![b]

Four Mysteries

[18]There are four marvelous mysteries
   that are[c] too amazing to unravel—
   who could fully explain them?[d]
[19]The way an eagle flies in the sky,[e]
   the way a snake glides on a boulder,[f]
   the path of a ship as it passes through the sea,[g]
   and the way a bridegroom falls in love with his bride.[h]

---

a 30:17As translated from the Septuagint.

b 30:17 This is a figure of speech for demonic powers that will remove their vision. Ravens and vultures are unclean birds associated with demonic powers in Hebrew poetry.

c 30:18 The Hebrew uses a poetic style of saying there are three mysteries, then saying there are four in order to emphasize their great importance. There could be within this poetic device a pointing to the fourth as the key, or the most important.

d 30:18 Notice that each of these four examples have to do with movement and mystery.

e 30:19 This is a picture of the overcoming life that soars above our problems and limitations with the wings of an eagle. It could also be a hint of the prophetic revelation that comes to God's servants mysteriously and supernaturally. See Isaiah 40:31 and 1 Corinthians 2:9–13.

f 30:19 The serpent becomes a picture of our sin that was placed on the Rock, Jesus Christ. See Numbers 21:6–9, John 3:14–15, and 2 Corinthians 5:21.

g 30:19 This is a picture of the way our lives, like a ship, sail on the high seas of mystery until we reach our destiny. Our lives contain mysteries, such as where God decided that we were to be born, how we were raised, and the companions who join us, until we reach our desired haven. See Psalm 107:23–30.

h 30:19 The Hebrew word translated "bride" can also mean "virgin," pointing to a wedding, thus implying the use of "bridegroom" instead of "man." (Consider Ruth and Boaz.) More important, this is a beautiful metaphor of the mystery of the love of our heavenly Bridegroom (Jesus), who romances his bride and sweeps us off our feet. Love is a mystery. See also 2 Corinthians 11:2 and Ephesians 5:32.

20Here is the deceptive way of the adulterous woman:[a]
    She takes what she wants and then says,
    "I've done nothing wrong."

Four Intolerable Things

21There are four intolerable events
    that[b] are simply unbearable to observe:
22When an unfaithful servant becomes a ruler,
    when a scoundrel comes into great wealth,
23When an unfaithful woman marries a good man,
    and when a mistress replaces a faithful wife.

Four Creatures Small and Wise

24The earth has four creatures that are very small but very wise:[c]
25The feeble ant has little strength,
    yet look how it diligently gathers its food in the summer
    to last throughout the winter.[d]
26The delicate rock-badger isn't all that strong,
    yet look how it makes a secure home, nestled in the rocks.[e]

---

a 30:20 The adulterous woman of Proverbs is a metaphor of the corrupt religious system. See Revelation 17–18.

b 30:21 See footnote for 30:18. These four events each depict a promotion undeserved, a displacing of one who is virtuous with one who is corrupt. Each promotion indicates that they will carry their corruption with them. The unfaithful servant will likely become a tyrant. The fool who becomes wealthy will squander his wealth. The unfaithful woman (or "hated woman") will continue her immorality even after she's married. The girlfriend who replaced the faithful wife will likely find another man one day.

c 30:24 Or "They are the epitome of wisdom."

d 30:25 To prepare for the future is a mark of true wisdom.

e 30:26 This becomes a picture of the believer. Though feeling weakness at times, we can make our home in the high place, inside the cleft of the Rock. See John 14:1–3.

²⁷The locusts have no king to lead them,
    yet they cooperate as they move forward by bands.ᵃ
²⁸And the small lizardᵇ is easy to catch
    as it clings to the walls with his hands,
    yet it can be found inside a king's palace.ᶜ

Four Stately Things

²⁹There are four stately monarchsᵈ
    who are impressive to watch as they go forth:
³⁰The lion, the king of the jungle, who is afraid of no one,
³¹The rooster strutting boldly among the hens,ᵉ
    the male goat out in front leading the herd,
    and a king leading his regal procession.ᶠ
³²If you've acted foolishly by drawing attention to yourself,
    or if you've thought about saying something stupid,
    you'd better shut your mouth.
³³For such stupidity may give you a bloody nose!ᵍ
    Stirring up an argument only leads to an angry confrontation.

---

a 30:27 The locust army points us to Joel 1 and 2. There is an awakening army coming to devour the works of the Enemy. Their King, though invisible, guides them from on high as one army.

b 30:28 Or "spider."

c 30:28 Though we may see ourselves as insignificant (like the small lizard), God can place us in significant places where we can be used for him.

d 30:29 See footnote on 30:18.

e 30:31 As translated from the Septuagint.

f 30:31 Or "a king surrounded by his band of soldiers." The Hebrew text is abstruse.

g 30:33 Or "Churning milk makes butter, and punching the nose brings blood, so stirring up anger produces quarrels." The Hebrew contains a word play with the word *anger*, which is almost identical to the word for "nose."

Proverbs 31

¹King Lemuel's[a] royal words of wisdom:
    These are the inspired words my mother taught me.[b]
²Listen, my dear son, son of my womb.
    You are the answer to my prayers, my son.
³So keep yourself sexually pure
    from the promiscuous, wayward woman.
    Don't waste the strength of your anointing
    on those who ruin kings—
    you'll live to regret it![c]
⁴For you are a king, Lemuel,
    and it's never fitting for a king to be drunk on wine
    or for rulers to crave alcohol.
⁵For when they drink they forget justice
    and ignore the rights of those in need,
    those who depend on you for leadership.[d]
⁶⁻⁷Strong drink is given to the terminally ill,
    who are suffering at the brink of death.
    Wine is for those in depression

---

a 31:1 Jewish legend is that King Lemuel was a pseudonym for Solomon, which would
    make his mother mentioned here to be Bathsheba. There is no other mention of Lemuel
    in the Scriptures. The Hebrew word translated "inspired words" is *massa*, which some
    have surmised was a place, meaning "Lemuel, King of Massa."

b 31:1 The Septuagint is "These are words spoken by God, and through a king came an
    answer divine."

c 31:3 As translated from the Septuagint.

d 31:5 Implied in the text.

in order to drown their sorrows.
Let them drink and forget their poverty and misery.
⁸But you are to be a king who speaks up on behalf
of the disenfranchised,
and pleads for the legal rights of the defenseless
and those who are dying.
⁹Be a righteous king, judging on behalf of the poor
and interceding for those most in need.ᵃ

The Radiant Bride

¹⁰Who could ever find a wife like this one—ᵇ
she is a woman of strength and mighty valor!ᶜ
She's full of wealth and wisdom,
the price paid for her was greaterᵈ than many jewels.
¹¹Her husband has entrusted his heart to her,ᵉ
For she brings him the rich spoils of victory.

---

a 31:9 See James 1:27.

b 31:10 Starting with verse 10 through the end of the book, we have a Hebrew acrostic
poem. It is alphabetical in structure, with each of the twenty-two verses beginning with
a consecutive Hebrew letter of the alphabet. The implication is that the perfections of
this woman would exhaust the entire language. The subject is the perfect bride, the
virtuous woman. This woman is both a picture of a virtuous wife and an incredible
allegory of the end-time victorious bride of Jesus Christ, full of virtue and grace.

c 31:10 The Hebrew word used to describe this virtuous wife is *khayil*. The meaning of this
word cannot be contained by one English equivalent word. It is often used in connection
with military prowess. This is a warring wife. *Khayil* can be translated "mighty; wealthy;
excellent; morally righteous; full of substance, integrity, abilities, and strength; mighty
like an army." The wife is a metaphor for the last-days church, the virtuous, overcoming
bride of Jesus Christ. The word *khayil* is most often used to describe valiant men. See
Exodus 18:21, where it is used for the mighty ones Moses was to commission as elders
and leaders among the people. Because many of the cultural terms and metaphors used
in this passage are not understood or even used in today's English-speaking world, the
translator has chosen to make them explicit.

d 31:10 Or "her worth." The price paid for her was the sacred blood of the Lamb of God,
her Bridegroom.

e 31:11 Or "has great confidence in her."

¹²All throughout her life she brings him what is good, and not evil.ᵃ
¹³She searches out continually to possess
   that which is pure and righteous.ᵇ
   She delights in the work of her hands.ᶜ
¹⁴She gives out revelation truthᵈ to feed others.
   She is like a trading ship bringing divine suppliesᵉ
   from the merchant.ᶠ
¹⁵Even in the night seasonᵍ she arisesʰ and sets food on the table
   for hungry ones in her house and for others.ⁱ
¹⁶She sets her heart upon a nationʲ and takes it as her own,

a 31:12 The virtuous bride will not bring disgrace to his name. Jesus will not be ashamed to display her to the world.

b 31:13 Or "wool and linen (flax)." Wool is a metaphor often used as a symbol of what is pure. See Isaiah 1:18, Daniel 7:9, and Revelation 1:14. Linen was made from flax and always speaks of righteousness. The priests of the Old Testament wore linen garments as they went before God's presence to offer sacrifices. The curtains of the tabernacle were likewise made of linen, signifying God's righteousness. See Exodus 28:39–43 and Revelation 19:8. The virtuous bride of Christ in the last days will be seeking for only what is pure and righteous in the eyes of her Bridegroom.

c 31:13 Or "eagerly works with her hands." The hands, with their five fingers, speak of the five ministries of the present work of Christ on the earth: apostles, prophets, evangelists, pastors, and teachers. These are often referred to as the five-fold ministries. Her delight is to equip others and help those in need.

d 31:14 Or "bread." This is a consistent emblem of spiritual food.

e 31:14 Or "supplies from far away." The implication is from another realm. She is bringing heavenly manna for those she feeds.

f 31:14 Or "like merchant ships bringing goods." Like a ship loaded with cargo, the bride of Christ brings heavenly treasures to others. The use of the term merchant points to Jesus Christ. He is described as a merchant in Matthew 13:45 in the parable of the costly pearl. The "pearl" is the church or the believer, which cost all that Jesus had (his blood) to purchase us.

g 31:15 She is interceding in the night, laboring in a night season to help others.

h 31:15 The Hebrew word translated "arise" can also mean "to rise up in power." We are told to "arise and shine, for our light has come." See Isaiah 60:1, which uses the same Hebrew word for "arise." The bride of Christ will arise with anointing to feed and bless the people of God.

i 31:15 Or "female servants." The servants are a metaphor of other churches and ministries.

j 31:16 Or "a land, a country."

carrying it within her.
She labors there to plant the living vines.[a]

[17]She wraps herself in strength,[b] might, and power in all her works.

[18]She tastes and experiences a better substance,[c]
and her shining light will not be extinguished,
no matter how dark the night.[d]

[19]She stretches out her hands to help the needy[e]
and she lays hold of the wheels of government.[f]

[20]She is known by her extravagant generosity to the poor,
for she always reaches out her hands[g] to those in need.

[21]She is not afraid of tribulation,[h]
for all her household is covered in the dual garments[i]
of righteousness and grace.

---

a 31:16 Or "By the fruit of her hands she plants a vineyard." (The Septuagint is "possession.") For the hands, see 31:13 footnote. This vineyard becomes a metaphor for the local church. We are the branches of the vine (Christ). See John 15. She is passionate about bringing forth fruit. She becomes a missionary to the nations, planting churches and bringing new life.

b 31:17 Or "She girds her loins with strength and makes her shoulders strong." This is a figure of speech for being anointed with power to do the works of Jesus. See John 14:12.

c 31:18 Or "good merchandise."

d 31:18 Her prayer life (lamp) overcomes her circumstances, even in a culture where darkness prevails.

e 31:19 As translated from the Septuagint. The Hebrew uses a term for "distaff" (a weaver's staff), which is taken from a root word for "prosperity." The poetic nuance of this phrase is that she uses her prosperity to bless the needy.

f 31:19 Or "Her hands grasp the spindle." The word translated as "spindle" can also mean "governmental circuits" or "wheels." There is a hint here of the wheels mentioned in Ezekiel 1. The throne of God's government sits on flaming wheels. See Daniel 7:9.

g 31:20 Notice the mention of her hands. See footnote on 31:13.

h 31:21 Or "snow." This is a figure of speech for the fear of a cold winter season.

i 31:21 As translated from the Septuagint. The Hebrew is "Everyone is covered in scarlet (blood)." Grace has brought righteousness to those in her house (under her ministry).

²²Her clothing is beautifully knit together^a—
    a purple gown of exquisite linen.
²³Her husband is famous and admired by all,
    sitting as the venerable judge of his people.^b
²⁴Even her works of righteousness^c
    she does^d for the benefit of her enemies.^e
²⁵Bold power and glorious majesty^f are wrapped around her
    as she laughs with joy over the latter days.^g
²⁶Her teachings are filled with wisdom and kindness,
    as loving instruction pours from her lips.^h
²⁷She watches over the ways of her householdⁱ
    and meets every need they have.
²⁸Her sons and daughters arise^j in one accord to extol her virtues,^k
    and her husband arises to speak of her in glowing terms.^l

---

a 31:22 This garment speaks of the ministries of the body of Christ, woven and knit together by the Holy Spirit. See Ephesians 4:15–16 and Colossians 2:2.

b 31:23 Or "sitting at the city gates among the elders of the land." Judgment was rendered at the gates of a city in that day. It was their courtroom. Our heavenly King is also the Judge. So famous, so glorious, yet he is our Bridegroom.

c 31:24 Or "linen." See footnote for 31:13 regarding linen as a symbol for righteousness.

d 31:24 Or "sells them." The root word for "sell" can also mean "surrender."

e 31:24 Or "aprons or belts for the Canaanites." The Canaanites were the traditional enemies of the Hebrews.

f 31:25 Or "beauty, honor and excellence."

g 31:25 The virtuous and victorious bride has no fear for the days to come. She contemplates eternity and her forever union with the Bridegroom.

h 31:26 The Septuagint is "She opens her mouth carefully and lawfully."

i 31:27 Or "She is a watchman over her house (family)."

j 31:28 The Hebrew word translated "arise" can also mean "to rise up with power." The Septuagint is "She raises her children so they will grow rich."

k 31:28 Or "Hooray, hooray for our mother!"

l 31:28 For more of how the heavenly Bridegroom loves his bride, read the Song of Songs.

²⁹"There are many valiant and noble ones,^{*a*}
  but you have ascended above them all!"^{*b*}
³⁰Charm can be misleading,
  and beauty is vain and so quickly fades,
  but this virtuous woman lives in the wonder, awe,
  and fear of the Lord.
  She will be praised throughout eternity.^{*c*}
³¹So go ahead and give her the credit that is due,
  for she has become a radiant woman,
  and all her loving works of righteousness deserve to be admired^{*d*}
  at the gateways of every city!

---

a 31:29 Or "Many daughters have obtained wealth because of her." These valiant and noble ones (daughters) represent the church of previous generations who remained faithful in their pursuit of Jesus. But this final generation will be the bridal company of the lovers of God who do mighty exploits and miracles on the earth.

b 31:29 Or "You are first in his eyes." See Song of Songs 6:8–9.

c 31:30 Implied in the context, supplied to complete Hebrew poetic parallelism.

d 31:31 The Septuagint could be translated, "Her husband is praised at the city gates."

About the Translator

Dr. Brian Simmons is known as a passionate lover of God. After a dramatic conversion to Christ, Brian knew that God was calling him to go to the unreached people of the world and present the gospel of God's grace to all who would listen. With his wife, Candice, and their three children, he spent nearly eight years in the tropical rain forest of the Darien Province of Panama as a church planter, translator, and consultant. Brian was involved in the Paya-Kuna New Testament translation project. He studied linguistics and Bible translation principles with New Tribes Mission. After their ministry in the jungle, Brian was instrumental in planting a thriving church in New England (U.S.), and now travels full time as a speaker and Bible teacher. He has been happily married to Candice for over forty-two years and is known to boast regularly of his children and grandchildren. Brian and Candice may be contacted at:

Facebook.com/passiontranslation
Twitter.com/tPtBible

For more information about the translation project or any of Brian's books, please visit:

thePassionTranslation.com
StairwayMinistries.org

Notes

Notes

Notes

Notes

Notes

Notes

Notes

Notes

Notes

Notes

Notes

Notes

Notes

Notes

thePassionTranslation.com